Crown of Victory

Crown of Victory

Dr. Adama Kalokoh

Impact Sierra Leone
Maryland

Crown of Victory
by Dr. Adama Kalokoh
Published 2025 by Impact Sierra Leone
Glen Burnie, Maryland 21061
www.impactsierraleone.org

©2025 by Dr. Adama Kalokoh

All rights reserved. No part of this book may be reproduced or transmitted in any form whatsoever without permission from the author except in the case of brief quotations embodied in articles, reviews, or books.

First Edition Published by Impact Sierra Leone

Printed in the United States of America
1 2 3 4 5 6 7 8 9 0

ISBN-13: 979-8-218-63682-1

Library of Congress Control Number: 2025904955

Editor: Ayanna Moo-Young

This book is dedicated to so many incredible people who in their own way shaped me as the woman I am today. To my beautiful mother, Madam Harriet Memuna Sesay, whose unspeakable courage during life's most difficult challenges taught me resiliency, built my character, and has been a constant reminder to never feel defeated. Mom, your witty sense of humor always reminds me to find joy on my journey and I am grateful for your undying love.

To my grandparents Pa Saidu Conteh, Pa Alhaji Sesay, Ya Adama Kamara and Ya Fatu Koroma, I thank you for your legacy. While I am saddened that I never met any of you alive, I am grateful to be your granddaughter and to carry your powerful legacy for generations to come.

To the men in my life who all left this world way too soon: My beloved father James Ibrahim Conteh, my younger brother Musa George Conteh, and elder brother Saidu Conteh, I dedicate this book to your memory. Each of you left me with sweet memories I will forever cherish. May your voices and legacies be honored always through my efforts. I especially thank my father for being one of my biggest inspirations and the why behind my love for doing humanitarian work in Sierra Leone.

I also dedicate this book to my amazing sisters: Fatmatta, Yeabu and Ramatu. Our bond is unbreakable and your presence in my life is a reminder that family is everything. I am proud that we each have dedicated ourselves to helping our motherland and bringing honor to our parents. We have all overcome so much but we still rise as beautiful daughters of Africa.

To my many friends all over the globe who have cheered me on even during the most unpredictable times, I thank you. Your support renews the meaning of my favorite saying, "We rise by lifting others."

To one very special being in my life who has shown me unconditional love, respect, and grace, I am extremely grateful for our bond- This King knows who he is, and I am thankful for you being part of my life journey.

I dedicate this book to my non-profit, Impact Sierra Leone. I am eternally grateful for the so many staff, volunteers, donors, supporters who have worked tirelessly to advance our mission. Collectively, we are making the world a better place by helping to reduce poverty, reduce hunger and spread hope. I am thankful for the many people in Sierra Leone whose resiliency and natural beauty reminds me there is always a reason to hope for a better tomorrow. To the children of Sierra Leone, especially the girls, your smiles of courage have always reminded me to be content no matter what the situation. This book is dedicated to the survivors, the overcomers, the unstoppable and those who have found victory by raising their voices for positive change.

Most importantly, this book is dedicated to God above for giving me strength and wisdom to write this book, even on the darkest of days. I thank God and credit him for all my blessings and success. I thank God for sending me helpers and mentors *who have poured into me all these years as a woman leader. I am grateful to God for the gift of life and his many provisions. I am filled with gratitude for my journey of impact which has truly given me wings of victory to soar towards my greatest destiny.*

Foreword by Kelly Markey

Award-Winning Author International Bestselling & Award-Winning Author CEO & Founder, Beacon of Hope Mission

In *Crown of Victory*, Dr Adama Kalokoh takes us on an extraordinary journey of self-discovery, resilience, and cultural awakening. Born to African parents, Adama navigated the complexities of her identity, battling insecurities related to her hair, skin, and her place within two worlds — the West and her ancestral homeland of Sierra Leone. Yet, through adversity, she found her strength and carved a path of purpose that has not only transformed her life but is now inspiring a generation.

This powerful memoir is more than a story of personal triumph; it is a testament to the human spirit's ability to rise above ridicule, loss, and rejection. From enduring the harsh realities of being misunderstood in her youth to serving in the military and ultimately reconnecting with her roots in Africa, Dr Kalokoh's story is one of grace, grit, and profound transformation. Her return to Sierra Leone ignited a deep passion to rewrite the narrative of her people and empower future generations, especially young girls born in villages with little hope.

Adama masterfully weaves the art of storytelling, drawing from her ancestors' wisdom and the strength of her ancestors to stand tall in her truth. With courage and compassion, she has become a beacon of hope, advocating for women's empowerment, and guiding young men toward a sustainable future. She reminds us that true leadership begins with finding our own voice before we can uplift others.

One of the most remarkable aspects of *Crown of Victory* is Dr. Adama's ability to turn pain into purpose. She gracefully honors those she lost in grief while carrying the torch of change forward. Her story is a powerful reminder that our scars are not signs of weakness but evidence of the battles we have conquered.

This book is not just an inspiring read; it is a call to action for those who dream of becoming changemakers, whether on a national or global scale. Adama's journey will stir your emotions, challenge your perspective, and ignite your own resilience and fortitude. And as a final gift, she invites readers to savor authentic recipes from Sierra Leone, offering a taste of her heritage and the culture that shaped her.

Crown of Victory is a celebration of identity, empowerment, and the unshakable spirit of a woman who turned her struggles into strength and her vision into impact. Dr Adama Kalokoh's voice is one that will echo through generations, leaving an indelible mark on hearts and communities across the globe.

This is not just a book; it is a movement — and I invite you to be part of it.

Contents

Preface i
Introduction 1
Culturally Rich 3
First-Generation Born 13
The Beauty of Colors 17
My Faith 23
Determination 31
Butterflies 37
Service 45
Travel to Sierra Leone 55
Seeds of History 65
The Journey of Impact 71
Voices of Impact 79
    The Voice of Change 79
    The Voice of Humanity - Adamsay 83
    The Voice of Talent - Alfred 89
    The Voice of Power - Huldah Imah Paul 92
    The Voice of Empowerment 99
I AM Adama 109
Conclusion 119
Bonus Recipes from Sierra Leone 123
    Krain Krain Soup 123
    Sierra Leonean Cassava Leaves 124
    Sierra Leonean Potato Leaves 125
    Okro or Okra Soup 127
    Jollof Rice 131
    Fufu 132
    Pepper Chicken 133

About the Author 137
    Honors 139
    Motivational Speaking Engagements 143
    Favorite Affirmations 146
Acknowledgements 149

Preface

This book has been long overdue and is a result of my determination to overcome life's many hurdles and distractions. I am a firm believer that we are all walking story books. We have many phases of our lives that represent a chapter: the good, bad and the ugly. These chapters shape who we are and what we become in society.

More importantly, we all have seeds that are planted within us from the very beginning which shape our character. From an agricultural perspective, seeds are placed in soil, watered, nurtured in the right environment, and sprout into plants. These plants produce fruit, vegetables, grain and even trees. For this reason, I am fascinated with seeds and have the utmost respect for farmers around the globe who, with much patience and care, contribute to food production and add value to the food chain. We are much like plants and must do our part to allow the seeds within us to grow so that we can reach our destinies.

There are so many seeds that have guided me: seeds of service, seeds of giving, and seeds of inspiring people. These seeds have been planted within me and have led me throughout my journey. Like many, I have had my share of joys, pains, triumphs, disappointments, setbacks, and comebacks. Yet, boldness and bravery are two attributes that helped me to write this book. I have always been told that I am a unique being with so much to share, but I had to realize this for myself. I had to embrace my voice and allow it to pull out my strength. This strength has led me to an even greater purpose. My journey excites me and scares me all at the same time. I hope that it will inspire you to never ever give up, to always reach higher, and to remember that there is something greater placed inside of you by God.

Introduction

Roy T. Bennett once quoted, "Accept yourself, love yourself, and keep moving forward. If you want to fly, you have to give up what weighs you down." This quote resonates with me. After accepting myself, loving myself truly, and moving forward towards my greatest destiny, I feel like a flying eagle every day, ready to conquer the world! If you have ever seen an eagle fly, then you know how powerful their wings are. You should become inspired to use the wings you have been given to soar to great heights.

For many years, I was silenced. Not by anyone else but, rather, the voice in my head which told me I was not good enough to be noticed. This same voice taunted that I was not the prettiest crayon in the box. It also told me that so many others were better than me in every way. But overtime, as I drew closer to God, I rediscovered who I was created to be, and I fell in love with myself all over again. I realized that despite my flaws, past, hurts, and regrets, I was still a magical masterpiece destined for greatness. During this discovery, I immersed myself in positive writings, images, affirmations, and quotes; and surrounded myself with positive people. During this time, my inner voice had a different tone and brought out a determination within me to succeed while being a light to others. I heard my inner voice this time around and realized I was more powerful than I thought. This voice of power ignited in me a desire to not only win but to triumph over all my troubles. I urge you to always search for the positive light in life; for this will be your greatest tool to not just survive in life but to thrive with power! Discovering my roots, my purpose, and my voice is what allowed me to be a huge inspiration to many around the world! Using my voice and embracing its power led me to become a nonprofit global leader.

    I look at my journey now and see that I have evolved from a shy, insecure young lady into a woman who is rooted in strong purpose and strength. I am what I am because of the sweet African soil. I proudly stand on the roots of my forefathers from Sierra Leone. This black skin, these high cheek bones, round hips and my unique name are a result of the beauty of a dignified people. I am forever grateful that I know where I come from. Join me in making Sierra Leone rise again!

Culturally Rich

I was born in the late 70's in an era when the world was crossing over from Motown music to the disco scene, and music videos would soon make their debut. My parents, Mr. James Conteh and Harriett Memuna Sesay, migrated to the United States in the late 1970's looking to better themselves and achieve the "American Dream". We lived in Washington, D.C. and I was the second of five children who are first-generation born African Americans. My parents, who both had roots in Yonibana, Sierra Leone, were connected through family prior to coming to the United States. Like many of their fellow Sierra Leonean counterparts, they sought to make a name for themselves within the African community.

My father was fortunate to attend one of the most prominent schools in Sierra Leone, Albert Academy, and because he excelled there, was later employed at the prestigious Rokel Commercial Bank in Kenema District. From there he was afforded the opportunity to travel to the United States where he became a successful engineer.

I've always admired my mother for her tenacity, hard work, and heart for helping others. She started a career in nursing while living in Sierra Leone. Her first visit to the United States was to New York, then she later settled in Washington, DC. She is the eldest of 14 children and the pride of her family. Her great sense of humor, wittiness, kindheartedness, and beautiful spirit are characteristics I've gratefully inherited.

Family Memories

My parents knew the value of hard work and did everything possible to make a great life for their children.

Like many families, we were not perfect and had many difficulties, but I truly cherish the time we spent growing up together.

Our household did not escape the traditions of Sierra Leone, as both of my parents retained their cultural practices including their culture, music and beliefs. They also retained their deep accents and spoke in their native tongues, Temne and Krio. I regret never learning these languages. They named all of us children after our grandparents. I am proudly the namesake for my maternal grandmother, Ya Adama Kamara, who was from the Ro' Konta village in the Northern Provinces of Sierra Leone.

We lived in a one-bedroom apartment, which today would seem small for a family of six, but I never knew I lacked. Our apartment number on Euclid Street was 115. My siblings and I had many adventures in that space. Playing Hide and Seek in our small apartment was the best. Trips to the grocery store always meant we would get our favorite candy bar which included Butterfinger, Peppermint Patties, KitKat, and Babe Ruth. In my earliest years, my mom threaded our hair beautifully and made all our clothing; we went to school dressed in colourful fabric dresses. We ate dinner on our corner table every night which varied from African rice dishes to fish sticks and fried chicken. I loved that my mom tried to cater to both American and African tastes in cuisine. An imitation picture of Mona Lisa hung on our wall and the brown leather recliner was designated only for my dad. When he came home from work, we all helped get his bags, took off his shoes, and served his plate. This was one benefit of having many girl children. My dad only ate African dishes with loads of African red pepper, which I could never tolerate.

Reading was fundamental in our home; we shared a bookcase loaded with a myriad of books. But before and after school, we watched our favorite television shows: The Jeffersons, Sanford and Son, Good Times, Laverne, and Shirley, Mork and Mindy, What's Happening, Amen, Happy Days, M.A.S.H, Cosby Show, Family Ties, 227, Different Strokes, I Dream of Jeannie, Bewitched, Miami Vice, Family Ties, Zoobilee Zoo, The Facts of Life, Reading Rainbow, Mr. Rogers, Care Bears, The Jetsons, The Flintstones, Scooby Doo and my all-time favorite, I Love Lucy. These shows made our childhood special, and we learned a lot about life from them as well.

Education and learning are very important to our family. My siblings and I walked to school each morning accompanied by our neighbor's older children, Selena and Godfrey. Not too long ago, I returned to my old neighborhood and took the route from our old apartment to my elementary school and realized we walked a very far distance! But as a child, it didn't seem as far, especially when we could stop at the candy store on the way to get Double Bubble Gum, Now and Later candy, and candy sticks.

The elementary school we attended, Marie H. Reed, was in the heart of Adam's Morgan and was known for its many international students. I had both memorable and miserable experiences there. Many teachers made my days special including my kindergarten teacher, Ms. Pride, my third-grade teacher, Ms. McCray, and my favorite, sixth grade teacher, Mr. Barron. His handwriting style coupled with my father's is why I have such beautiful penmanship to this day. We wore uniforms, green-blue plaid bottoms and white shirts.

One summer, my two sisters and I joined a summer reading contest at the Petworth Neighborhood Library. While other kids were at the pool, we raced to the library each day to read the most books and by no surprise, we won. The prize, of course, was brand new books for each category won, an achievement certificate and bragging rights.

I was involved in many activities, but what I excelled most in was the Spelling Bee. In fact, all my siblings were involved in the Spelling Bee and won several times. We were known as the Conteh sisters. My sister and I competed in the Regional Spelling Bee which was televised by Channel NBC and garnered so much respect from our peers.

In addition to expanding my vocabulary, I developed leadership skills as a proud safety patrol. I wore my bright orange shoulder clip belt with pride as I ushered my fellow peers in the crosswalk.

Our babysitter was a grandmother figure known to us only as "Mama". In many ways, she was more like the grandmother we never had. I'm not sure how our African parents stumbled across her, but it made sense because other African kids went there as well. Mama took care of us as if we were her very own grandchildren. My dad dropped us off some early school mornings and Mama would make us a hearty country breakfast every time and ensure we looked neat as we left for school. My parents also dropped us off to her if they were attending a party during the weekend. There were many interesting characters in her home. As I am older, I realize some of these characters had no business around children, not because they were dangerous but because they were always reeking of alcohol. Nonetheless, Mama was our Mama Bear and had her eye on every single child.

One fond memory I have is of the early morning gospel songs she would play. I believe this is where my appreciation for gospel songs developed. These three songs were always playing at Mama's house: "Everything Is Going to Be Alright" by Al Green; "Rough Side" of the Mountain by Rev F.C Brown and Rev Janice Brown; and "You Brought the Sunshine" by the Clark Sisters. To this day, anytime I hear these songs on the radio, I instantly think about Mama and those sweet mornings before school. Even at the young age of seven, I had an appreciation for these songs and their beautiful rhythmic beats.

The weekends were extra special. We frequented the playground, especially on hot summer days. Our favorite playtime memories were at Malcolm X Park which was both creepy and thrilling at the same time. It was surrounded by huge statues of lions and other animals. It was also surrounded by lots of water that I swam in once or twice. My siblings and I were most entertained by the popular tv shows at the time. We watched Soul Train, American Bandstand and Solid Gold as we sat on our favorite floral couch. When we were not watching the music shows, we were listening to them on my dad's record player. Every Saturday, the record player spun while Mom prepared the delicious soup of the day. My dad had a vast collection of albums including several Michael Jackson albums, R&B oldies, and plenty of African oldies. On Saturdays, we listened to songs and danced.

I got my first taste of humanitarian service as a little girl witnessing the Saturday gatherings of Sacoma, a group comprising many of our aunts and uncles that met at our place to serve as a network for all the Sierra Leone migrants in the DC area, particularly those from Yonibana. Our house was filled with our relatives all speaking the same dialect with such animation. My father was an active member of this organization and always believed that you should help those who were less fortunate. The aroma of sweet plantains and potato leaves soup, my two favorite dishes, filled the room. My mother was a supportive member who cooked all the meals for these Saturday meetings. I marveled at how everyone used their voices powerfully to state the needs within our community, especially my own father. My inner self secretly desired to be equally as passionate for a cause someday.

My parents were my first mentors who encouraged me to always follow my heart. They always inspired me and my siblings to not only work hard, but to make sure we help others along the way. They planted a desire in me to serve at a young age. Their hard work as immigrants to the U.S was very admirable, and I vowed to ensure their labor would not be in vain.

First-Generation Born

Growing up brought some joy, some pain, and a lot of confusion in between. Naturally, my parents ensured to pass all their cultural practices to their American-born children. Whether we fully accepted their traditions was another story! Children who are first-generation born are often stuck in the middle of our identity. I dare not call it identity crisis, more like identity confusion. I thought I had to choose between my African roots and my being born and raised in America. At times, I felt ashamed or embarrassed and went through a phase in which I just wanted to identify as being a Black American. As I met people and spoke of my heritage, I only shared the parts I thought the receiver would embrace.

My name was Adama Conteh. By the third grade, this along with the beautiful dresses my mother made for me became the subject of tease. It's not that my name was difficult to pronounce but it always drew questions like, "Is your dad named Adam?" There was emphasis on the wrong syllables even after I corrected the mispronunciation. For many years I allowed my name to be pronounced incorrectly. I was always embarrassed during awards ceremonies because my name was frequently mispronounced. On graduation day, I received so many awards but inside felt too self-conscious to get up and receive them. I tried to fit in at all costs which meant abandoning my true self on many occasions, even to the extent of changing my name to the likes of Dominique or Maria just to please my peers. It wasn't until 2003 when I travelled to Sierra Leone for the first time that I learned that not only was I named after my maternal grandmother, but my name was also considered the Muslim version of Adam meaning queen, mother of the earth. There is so much power in knowing the meaning of your name. From the moment that I discovered my name carried meaning of a Queen, I seemed to raise my shoulders a bit higher and unapologetically carried myself like royalty. I urge everyone to always remember the power of your name, its meaning, and its roots.

    I never liked going to school wide activities because I hated the limelight. At my sixth-grade graduation, I was the only girl not in pastel although the teachers stressed the strict dress code. My mom bought what was on sale and although I didn't understand at the time, she did all she could with love. Besides my cultural differences, I was ridiculed for the appearance of my smile and teeth. I had a terrible finger sucking habit until I was about age 12 that caused me to have an overbite. This imperfection made me avoid talking as much as possible but ironically, I loved to laugh. I was convinced that due to my imperfect looks, I had little to say to the world. I wanted to draw as little attention to myself as possible. This is hard to do when you look uncommon and have an uncommon name.

Thank goodness I had an outlet as a member of the band. I was a trumpet player. I made our home noisy with all my practice but my love for music followed me to my junior high school, Shaw. Once in attendance, it was not long before I joined the Shaw marching band, playing the clarinet. We performed at many big events in D.C. and even traveled to other states. I wore my green, white, and yellow band uniform with pride: white hat, white shoes and white socks that went with each uniform. I can still see my mom's face as I suited up for a performance, especially our winter concerts. "Shaw time is showtime so let's get busy!" This was our oh so famous slogan as we began performances. We played popular songs of that time and were known as one of the best bands around. We even performed at the Cherry Blossom Parade.

I never felt fully accepted by either the American culture or African culture. As I got older, I became accustomed to telling people I was from Washington D.C., knowing that my African roots were a major part of my life story. I was often confused which culture to claim and at the right times. Yes, of course, attending African functions with my African parents put me in front of relatives who dubbed us as African kids. But outside of functions or places where people knew my family, a lot of people were confused where I fit in on the cultural map. Many who met me along the way would ask, "Where are you from?" I would boldly and proudly say, "I was born and raised in DC." This response left most of them perplexed and they'd usually followed up with another comment like, "Oh really, you look like you come from another country, your features stand out." Then I would provide part two of my response: "Oh yeah, my parents are from Sierra Leone, but I was born in the United States." I always placed heavy emphasis that my parents are from Africa but I'm not from Africa. Later in life, after lots of maturity, I realized I couldn't separate the two - I was simply African American and needed not to be ashamed. Today, I confidently share that I am a proud descendant of Sierra Leone, West Africa and, thus, classify my identity as a combination of American and African. Through both cultures, I developed a strong passion for helping others and international development.

The Beauty of Colors

During my early years of school, I also discovered the colour phenomenon, "light-skinned" vs "dark-skinned", which now I know was propaganda to separate us as a people. Colourism amongst African Americans can be traced back as far as slavery. It made me angry at times to think about how our beautiful, different shades should've encouraged us to embrace one another instead of separating us even more.

I grew up in the Washington D.C. area during the 1980s in an area considered a melting pot of diversity, so I thought. This is where I developed deep insecurities and experienced some of the ugliest hatred amongst my own African American people.

At school, the terms light- skinned, brown-skinned, and dark-skinned were some of the main descriptors students used to characterize their peers. My first encounter with this colour system was around second grade and it really hit home in the third grade: "You are too black for us to see your baby hairs." I vividly remember this statement from another third grader as we assembled in the bathroom for a break. I chuckled with the other girls but deep down inside, I was crying out in pain. It's amazing that after all these years, I can remember this moment as if it was yesterday. "What is wrong with my black skin?" I pondered. Little did I know it would become something that would taunt me throughout my youth. Moments such as these led me to many years of self-doubt and insecurity, believing my black was not beautiful.

Being "dark-skinned" was not popular. The young boys catcalled the girls by their complexions: "Hey black, hey red …" or they referred to them as the light-skinned girl, brown-skinned girl, or dark-skinned girl. Most often when I overheard their gestures, the light-skinned girl was described as pretty and cute while dark-skinned one was just "alright" but in many cases, "the ugly one". The scale of beauty for the two colours was uneven; the light-skinned girl was always leading the way and being chosen. The biggest lie that was planted in our heads was that dark-skinned was less than, imperfect and less intelligent, whereas light-skinned individuals were instantaneously stamped pretty and smart.

It seemed that if you were light in complexion with "good" textured hair, you were in the cool kid club. As I think about it, this concept of good hair has been such a controversy. Ever since the creation of the hair perm and even the straightening comb, it created the illusion that if your hair was not silky straight and easy to comb, it was considered nappy or not good. Several periods in African American history show entertainers and high-profile individuals going from their original thick, curly hair to wearing their hair straight which had such a heavy influence on normal everyday people. This relates back to my previous references about light-skinned vs. dark-skinned. "Good hair" is synonymous with hair that looks acceptable to society and is closer to our Caucasian counterparts. I'll admit, I fed into this notion of wanting straighter hair and when I was about 12 years old, received my first relaxer. I felt so pretty after seeing my hair straightened out and never wanted to return to my thick nappy hair. It was easier to comb than my natural, curly coils. One day I was watching the Little Rascals on television, a popular show with a Black character named Buckwheat, a little boy with nappy hair. In fact, I was called Buckwheat many times because of my dark skin and thick hair. When I was out with friends and we saw a baby or toddler with curly hair, the first thing one of my friends would say is, "Oh, he or she got good hair." It wasn't until years later that I realized there is no such thing as good hair and that our true beauty comes from within.

  Nonetheless, I started believing that being dark-skinned was not good enough. So, because of these negative labels and lots of teasing, I grew up feeling less beautiful and unexcited about being of African descent. I no longer enjoyed my mother's traditional braiding hairstyles or dressing up in traditional outfits. I wanted so much to fit into the American crowd and spare myself anymore embarrassment. I wanted to erase any connection with Africa because I truly felt my black was not beautiful. The experience of being teased made me extremely shy and eager to erase anything that revealed my African background, including my name.

I did all I could to fit in with the crowd and cool kids. I tried hard to make people laugh so that at least they could see my charm. Unfortunately, this did not prevent the teasing, so I got used to being called dark-skinned, ugly and many other negative monikers.

This color code was enforced by other races that also discriminate against us, and this occurs even in today's time. In Hollywood, great dark-skinned actors and actresses are often overlooked for roles that are given to their light-skinned counterparts. What's interesting and disheartening is that I later discovered this colourism also existed in the Motherland. Many pigmented people have drowned themselves in lighting cream because they've accepted the false notion that light-skinned is more beautiful. Much of this is exacerbated by western civilization's belief since it has such a heavy influence on the people in Africa, especially nowadays due to access via social media.

Ironically, as I got much older it almost seemed like the colourism faded. I began to receive many compliments on my skin color. Because I wasn't accustomed hearing kind words about it, I didn't know how to accept the compliment. Going from being someone who learned to hate her dark skin because she was ridiculed for it to suddenly receiving compliments challenged my beliefs. How was I now supposed to fall in love with my black skin?

I didn't truly adore my skin until my father passed in 1997. My father had a beautiful skin color, almost as if the sun personally kissed on his cheeks. It was quite a journey to get to my level of self-love I have today. The Adama you see today went through layers of hurt, but diamonds must go through pressure to get that right spark. Surrounding myself with likeminded, mature individuals who embraced diversity made a huge difference. Exposure to other cultures and people is a key solution to ignorance. It feels good to love who God created me to be and I am not turning back.

If you are questioning your beauty because of your skin color, I encourage you to look deep within yourself and remember how we are all a part of the beautiful rainbow of colors. Your uniqueness is your superpower. We are all beautiful in God's eyes. Finding the positive voice within and channelling it into every moment of your life will keep you going on your journey to success.

My Faith

Seeds of faith were planted in me by my parents at an early age. My mother shared her experiences with us. As the eldest of 14 children, there was so much pressure on her to make it big. She was born into a strict Muslim family where her father (my grandfather) was a popular Imam who had gone to Mecca. She went to Arabic school and knew the traditional Muslim prayers as did most of the Muslim children. She eventually attended a Catholic boarding school. Surprisingly, her father did not give her difficulty, considering Catholicism was not his faith. He had also been influenced by Christianity while in Sierra Leone although he was Muslim. He was more focused on her getting the best education possible. The nuns had a heavy influence on her spiritual journey.

Naturally this influence followed both parents when they migrated to the United States.

In the United States, my parents joined the Methodist church, and my siblings and I attended the Calvary Methodist Church Pre-school during our pre-kindergarten years. We faithfully attended church every Sunday. I remember those hard wooden pews, row by row with the distinct, burgundy-cushioned altar in the front. A Bible and hymnal sat on every pew, although it seemed we sang the same songs every Sunday. We all entered the sanctuary dressed in our best Sunday outfits, and we sat in the same place in the middle pews. My mother loved to tell us bible stories especially about John and Mary. She took pride in making sure we looked our best for church services, especially during the Christian holidays. We were always so pristine in our Sunday dresses and shoes. It always seemed dark inside the church. The ceilings were super-high, and the walls were adorned with images of White Jesus all around.

    While we knew not to act out at church, there were days of exceptions when my siblings and I threw paper at each other and found an excuse to pick up an unnecessary object on the floor. We did everything to speed up the time as we awaited the call for all the youth to head to Sunday School service. Finally, we could let loose, be free, and have fun, so we thought. The Sunday School teacher was very strict but that didn't prevent me from cracking jokes and making the other kids laugh. Sunday school was a great foundation for my learning about the Bible and God. But one thing's for sure, my jovial character impressed all the children; I was known as the jokester, putting laughter into what would be a somewhat boring bible lesson.

My favorite moments at church were during the holidays: Christmas parties, Easter egg hunts, Thanksgiving harvest meals, so many sweet memories. One fine Sunday, we were all baptized, sprinkled with holy water. That day, there was a surprise celebration planned for us when we returned home. The taste of sweet acara and plantains is still in my mouth. This upbringing taught me that having faith as a Christian meant you must be dedicated.

Interestingly, during every African occasion in which the Muslim prayer was being recited, both my parents still recited the verses perfectly. When I questioned my mom about it one day, she simply said: "Although I am a Christian, my respect for the Muslim faith will always be there because of our culture and family roots."

These seeds of faith have carried me throughout my life journey. As I grew older and our family dynamics changed, my faith in God was often shaky but I did not lose my anchor in Christ. During my pre-teen years, my parents split, and we were officially a single-parent household. As a result, we moved around a lot and did not have a stable church home. It was a very confusing time for our family. One thing that I am grateful for is that even as a teenager, I was devoted to the principles of Christ and doing what is right. My younger brother Musa suffered the most by not having the experience of both parents nurturing him as a young man. Though we were not physically meeting in church, we never ceased in our daily prayers.

After some time, I started longing for a church home. One summer day as my sisters and I were playing in the street, a beautiful soul, Sister Whitehead, approached us and invited us to Vacation Bible School. We were new to the neighborhood and often went to nearby play areas to have fun. Sister Whitehead mentioned that this Christian day camp was free to attend, would be fun, and provided free meals, so we went home and excitedly told my mother. Within a few months, we were regularly attending Zion Hill Baptist Church.

The church had burgundy pews with "Zion Hill Baptist Church" branded fans inside the sleeves that you were not supposed to take home. The ushers greeted you at the door wearing white dresses and shoes. Unlike the methodist church that had a clockwork start and end time, there were times the services at Zion Hill went into overtime. They even had second services. One of my special memories at this church was the delicious food served on special occasions. The theme was always "soul food" which made attending a second service on Sunday a challenge to stay awake. I also enjoyed when we had a guest preacher. The singing was very soulful and rhythmic. I joined the choir as one of the altos.

The baptismal pew was right behind the podium where the pastor preached. We began going to Vacation Bible School but eventually took the faithful walk wearing our white clothing into the baptismal pool, fully immersed. On the day of the baptism, the women prepared and adorned me in an all-white outfit and socks while singing, "Come to Jesus". I can't remember the exact date, but I know it was around the age of 13 when the pastor said: "I now baptize you in the name of the Father, Son, and the Holy Spirit!" I quickly attended New Members Class but realized I really didn't know how to effectively study the bible. It didn't seem practical for me but over time, I started finding scriptures that I could hold onto as I grew into my teenage years. We were involved in so many activities including youth choir, youth usher team, communion team and much more. Joining this church was very timely as I entered my teenage years and experienced much more peer pressure. It was because of this church that I protected my virginity with so much care and thankfully did not fall into pre-marital sex. Our Sunday school sessions focused on the popular teenage struggles including teenage drinking, sex, partying, etc. The information presented at Sunday School frightened me enough to not even think about going outside of God's will. Every class gave a take home material with stories and lots of scriptures on obedience to God. I quickly learned a phrase often preached in the church which always rang loudly in my ears: There was a hell waiting for me and I would "go to hell in a handbasket" if I fell into these sins. During our teen Bible study, we shared a lot of what was happening in our lives and these discussions were a great outlet for me. This coupled with scriptures provided the spiritual guidance needed.

I attended a Christian Camp called Young Life with the church youth. We traveled to the camp via bus with children from many area churches. My best friend, who also attended Zion Hill, accompanied me along with her boyfriend. Their company eased my anxieties from being around the children from other churches. I'll admit, it was awkward to witness my friend receiving affection from her guy, but nonetheless, they were my comfort zone. I thought I would not have any insecurities because I was surrounded by youth who knew Christ. This was far from the truth. But there were some joyous moments during the camp, especially the group singing. The songs we sang at this camp still ring in my head. While at this camp, I met a handsome young man named Cody, the first guy who paid me any attention, although this lasted only a moment.

There I was going on the Zipline water slide with Cody watching along the side. In a bizarre twist, I ziplined farther than I needed and submerged into the water. I saw my life flash before my very eyes. I began screaming loud bear sounds that people on the other side could hear. Unfortunately, the lifeguards were not attentive. My guardian angel, Cody, jumped in fully clothed to save me from drowning. I was relieved and embarrassed at the same time. Cody was given a certificate during our camp assembly, and I was also asked to stand, as if I was not ashamed enough. This camp made me realize that I was not a swimmer, although I had taken swimming lessons earlier that year. I was a testament that panicking can take any of your swimming skills away in just a snap.

I did not hear from Cody again after this camp, which made this my first experience of teenage heartbreak but certainly not my last.

Determination

I am a firm believer that God has an objective for our plans, a motive for our struggles and a gift for our faithfulness. These words have been a driving force for me to be determined and to never give up while on this journey called life. I was a very strong-willed young woman from early age. My main goal was to make my parents proud, especially my mom, knowing the difficulties immigrants face when they come to the United States. Moving to a distant country far from family, I saw my parents work hard to provide their children with better opportunities firsthand. My mother was a dedicated nurse and worked many shifts, sometimes double shifts, to make sure we did not lack anything. When she picked us up from the after-school program at Marie H. Reed Elementary, she was very exhausted. My father was a brilliant engineer and worked for Martin's Chevrolet. Both parents reminded us daily to be the best students we can be and to make them proud. The pride of every African parent, especially those from Sierre Leone, is to have a child who is well-educated and excels in school. In fact, it is their children who they boast about when seeing their fellow Sierra Leoneans. As a child of an immigrant, I was determined to excel in everything I did which is why I was involved in many school clubs and activities. This determination carried over to my junior high and high school days.

It was such an honor to be chosen into the Wilson International Special Program (WISP) at Wilson Senior High School, home of the Tigers. I took advanced classes, including AP Spanish. Although I was very intelligent, I held onto the intense insecurity that was born during my earlier years regarding my not so perfect smile. During class, I was extremely shy and quiet. I wanted to excel behind the scenes. There were times I would be called on to read something in class and it would cause my stomach to sink. It made it extremely difficult for me to relate to boys. Having a boyfriend or any male admirer during that time was totally out of the question. I grew accustomed to seeing my fellow girlfriends interact with male friends while I stood at a distance, very quiet. I knew where I stood on the high school social map.

During my 11th-grade year in high school, I got a job working at Kentucky Fried Chicken (KFC) as a cashier in the Howard University area and worked there after school and on the weekends as needed. The job provided exposure to older people who helped me mature quickly; not to mention, it provided much needed financial support. I paid for most of my senior year activities with this job, so it meant a great deal. I learned to have more patience as well. I was determined to work hard, be nice to all customers and be the best worker. My intentions were great but that did not prevent people from making cruel remarks because of my overbite and dark skin. Many of our customers were Howard University students, some who were still not fully mature in their thinking. I determined myself not to let anyone break my spirit, change my positive attitude, or diminish me as a person. What shocked me the most was many of the disparaging remarks regarding my skin color came from customers who were African American. Were we not all black but just different shades? I remember walking home many nights almost in tears from some hurtful comments. What's bizarre is that I also received many compliments from customers for my beauty, but I never replayed these in my head. I most remembered the cruel comments; they played in my head repeatedly. Some days, I thought it'd be better to just quit instead of facing such cruelty daily. But the seed of determination within me would not let me quit. I persevered and dug deeper in my faith which reminded me that I was God's masterpiece.

My need to have a sense of belonging led me to join the Junior Reserve Officer Training Corps (JROTC). I was on the Unarmed Drill Team, and we competed against other area schools and won a few competitions. Although I also had been teased by my fellow drill members, I had built a resilient inner strength which taught me how to easily ignore the haters.

The pressure to be perfect in high school is absolutely no joke. But the best way to attack this is to love yourself deeply, to develop healthy mindset habits and great friendships where your outer self is not the first thing that is judged. My mental toughness developed the most during this period. I built enough confidence to run for "Most Likely to Succeed" although I did not win. Just my effort to run showed I had come a long way from my insecurity. I knew I would succeed and did not need a high school label as approval.

My graduation day was such a proud moment in my life. I started preparing very early in the morning at a neighborhood beauty salon. I got my hair styled in some fancy finger waves for the special occasion. This was a popular hairdo, and I wanted to be in the cool kids' club on my special day. My parents both wore their traditional African attire representing the Sierra Leone culture. My dad showed up in his royal blue Agbada outfit and his signature smile. After graduation, relatives gathered at our home where I danced my last dance with my father to the song,

"My Identity" by Burning Spears. This song would forever take on a different meaning.

Butterflies

Butterflies are the most fascinating and magnificent insects God ever created. They start their transition from crawling caterpillars and then become beautiful creatures with delicate features, using their wings to soar with the wind. I stand in awe every time I see one. They are my favorite insects because they represent powerful change as they transform from caterpillars to beautiful, winged butterflies. These beautiful creatures go through transformation to become something greater. It begins its journey in a humble state as a caterpillar and over time, with patience and nature's nectar, it grows beautiful wings that help it to soar to the highest heights. They are one of a kind in design, but all have one thing in common: they don't stop moving. They continue soaring wherever their wings take them on their journey. Whenever you see one, stop and watch it soar; look at its wings and be inspired. As you will read further in this chapter, butterflies always remind me of my father.

One of my fondest childhood memories I cherish most is when I turned the age of 10. On one beautiful day in

May, my birthday to be exact, I was led by my father to a great surprise birthday party in the park in my honor. The park, Malcolm X Park in Washington D.C., was one of our favorite places to go for enjoyment. I vividly remember the look of love on his face when he saw my eyes light up with happiness. He whispered, "Yes, this is for you Adama." On that day, I felt like the African Princess my father constantly called us as his daughters. He was the one man that constantly told me that I was beautiful and how super proud he was of me. At that moment, there were seeds planted in me to keep my head up and believe in a greater future. During my painful moments of insecurity, I could hear the voice of my father reminding me that I was a beautiful African princess.

    My high school graduation was the last celebratory event my father was alive. My life dramatically changed forever when on May 8, 1997, at approximately 8:35pm, my father, James Ibrahim Conteh, passed away. I held onto the phone for over 45 minutes waiting to speak to my dad, only for the doctor to come on and announce that he had just passed. I was so devastated. I felt my voice shatter because I now had to make the phone call to my family. It was a stormy day but even the thunder could not drown out my agonizing screams from my military dorm room. After being comforted from other airmen from my dormitory, I mustered up enough courage to use my voice and utter the bitter news to my mother. Before I could even say a word, she already knew something tragic had happened and pleaded with me to get home right away. This was a day I will never ever forget because I truly thought at the young age of 19, I could not possibly go on to do great things with such heavy pains. I was extremely close with my father and always imagined him walking me down the aisle to marry a man of God someday.

One of my last memories with my father was during my high school graduation. I had a quiet moment with my father as we were taking pictures and he reminded me that not only did I make him proud, but I also made all my family members in Sierra Leone proud. My heart was overjoyed because I knew at that moment, he was most proud to be my father, and I, his daughter.

My father's death left such an emptiness in me, a void that I felt could never be filled. I would take long walks on the military base hoping that I could hear his voice in the wind, trying to find peace. I cried constantly just remembering his last days and the last words I uttered to him while visiting him in the hospital, "Daddy, I'm coming back to see you, ok?" I can also remember the last time I physically touched my father. I applied Blistex lip balm to his lips and said, "I Love You." That moment stayed in my head for months and always accompanied tears of regret that I didn't do enough. But then one day, as if God himself decided it was time for you to feel peace, as I was walking on base crying, I saw the most beautiful butterfly covered in my favorite color, blue. I stopped in awe to watch it as it flew in the air. In that moment, in the stillness, I could hear God say, "It is well." I felt my father's presence as the butterfly soared around, and I knew this was somehow my father also saying to me, "Adama, it is well." From then on, seeing a butterfly took on a whole new meaning. Smiles of joy and peace replaced my tears of sadness. To this day, when I see a butterfly, I look to the sky and say, "Yes Daddy, it is well." When the death of a loved one hits you, there is no one size fit all for healing. You must find your own way of moving forward while keeping the memory of them alive. What was previously just a butterfly had become my "butterfly blessing".

Some of the most memorable features of my father were his dark almond eyes and curly eyelashes. I inherited these features and much like him, I smile with my eyes. His eyes revealed strength, beauty, pain, passion, and joy but also deep love. My father loved his country Sierra Leone and never stopped sharing stories with his children. He painted a picture of Sierra Leone that I still hope to see become a full reality.

My Smile From U

Another member of my family that I wish I could snap my fingers and return to earth is my baby brother, Musa George Conteh. As painful as it is, I cannot complete this book without mentioning my brother and the impact he had on my life. My baby brother was the last of the Conteh siblings born in the United States and the only boy. I was eight years old when he was brought home from the hospital. My sisters and I all became his mother which probably frustrated him a lot in life. I felt the closest to him and understood his plight of striving to become a man despite not really growing up with our dad in his life.

Musa was such a character and had a witty sense of humor. I remember taking him to the daycare and picking him up every day just as if I was his mother. We had a very special bond, and I often felt as though he was my first-born child.

I try to remember the good memories as part of my healing journey because his death was very crippling. He and my other two siblings came to visit me while I was stationed at Andrew's Air Force Base. They felt so proud that their big sister was officially in the military, and I was happy to take them on a tour of the base. Musa was fascinated by my military uniform, from my boots to my Battle Dress Uniform (BDUs). We took many pictures during this trip and did what we loved most; we danced! We watched one of our favorite movies together called the "Temptations" repeatedly. I can still feel the laughter from that special moment.

I now realize the value and importance of treasuring each moment you have with your loved ones. I am an African butterfly soaring every day to a great purpose. We all start off as caterpillars, trying to figure out our purpose in life. We were born to thrive and not just survive in this world. No matter your story, you are equipped with unique talents and skills to succeed. Use everything inside of you as your wings to soar above to the greatest height of success. Keep soaring and remember your worth! I hope you are inspired to look within and embrace those unique skills that will set you apart from others in your field. Work towards your professional development each and every day and inspire the world! When you discover your purpose then you will find your voice and truly be unstoppable.

Service

I began military service in high school when I joined the Junior Reserve Officer Training Corps (JROTC) program and was a proud junior cadet, learning the ropes and being taught about commitment and being set apart. We were required to wear our uniforms twice a week with neatly pressed shirts, creased pants, and shined shoes. Those olive-green uniforms were not the fanciest, but they sure gave us a sense of importance amongst our peers. We performed at high school military drills with precision. Our instructors had all served in various branches of the military but there was heavy Army influence. Military recruiters were frequent visitors looking for their best recruits into the military. They caught most of our attention when they shared how the military would help pay for our college education, allow us to travel the world and make good steady income if we joined. For someone like me who lived in the home with many siblings and was insecure about the financial means to attend a four-year college, tuition perks really piqued my interest.

I also heard that to enjoy these perks, you had to be willing to sacrifice your life and endure six intensive weeks of basic training. This made me uncertain, so I pursued scholarships from area colleges and universities. Afterall, my grades were decent, and I was involved in noteworthy school activities that would look good on my college application. So, there I was, putting my idea of going into the military on hold and shifting my energy into the grueling process of filling out college applications. But migraines, and a lack of mentorship and guidance made it difficult to complete a solid application. My goal was to receive a full scholarship but, unfortunately, this was not my fate. Words matter when it comes to articulating your value as a candidate for a scholarship. Through my love for children and helping people, I applied to Hampton University as a potential candidate for their pediatrician nursing program. However, I was only awarded a partial scholarship, and I began to doubt my future. I thought to myself, "How awful it would be to begin college only to struggle to pay tuition each semester and not be able to finish." I am a person that hates starting something I cannot finish. So, I went back to my original option of joining the military. After much contemplation, prayer, and influence from other JROTC members, I finally made the decision to join the military, the Army to be specific.

  When the recruiter came to our house to talk to my mom, she went into full African mom mode, telling the recruiter to make sure he didn't allow anything to happen to her child. Little did she know that recruiter's job ended once I left for basic training. I was 19 years old at the time and the prayers of my mother and church family were my saving grace. My life was totally in the hands of God from then on.

Interestingly, after signing up to join the Army, I was informed that I would have to take a one-week training course which involved jumping from an airplane. I switched to the Air Force at the very last minute. Instead of heading to Fort Sam Houston for Army basic training, I headed to Lackland Air Force Base for training. The day before I left for basic training, I lodged in a hotel and the song that played on the radio was, "I Believe I Can Fly". I felt so much peace in my decision and a strong feeling that my life would never be the same ever again. Boy was that true!

It was a chilly day on November 20,1996 when I said my final farewell to my family as I left for the Air Force, boarding a plane for the very first time in my life, taking the long journey to Texas from Washington D.C. I braided my hair in the popular bob-style braids and felt ready for whatever was ahead. As we arrived at Lackland Air Force Base, surrounded by so many other future airmen, I took a solemn oath with my right hand up to defend my country with dignity and respect. I didn't know these same beautiful bob-style braids would draw the wrong attention from my military instructors. I was one of nine Black cadets out of fifty-four women airmen and my braids made me a target.

The next two months of my life would prove to be the most challenging as I fought past all barriers just to complete basic training without giving up. If it was not the physical fitness days on Mondays, Wednesdays, and Fridays which I dreaded, or the early morning start of our days, then it was the constant yelling from the training instructors and the longing to see my family again. The first week was considered "0" week and was filled with intense mental as well as emotional stress. I nearly gave in to returning home in peace but the fighter in me was ignited. As the weeks went on, I felt a strong sense of pride knowing I was also making my family so proud.

My decision to join the military as a woman was not popular amongst my parents and relatives, but this later changed further into my military career. The military was all about order and discipline. Making beds with rulers, precision in uniform presentation, walking in cadence with my platoon, shining boots with perfection, surviving a difficult obstacle course, and firing my first rifle were all a part of the programming. The physical demand was so gruesome. Pushups, sit-ups and running laps were our core exercises. By the end of basic training, I was a size 8 with abs that I could see in the flesh. There were also lots of adventures including our training overnight in the wilderness. The bear encounters were memorable, and so was the joy of receiving letters and care packages from family. I received care packages and letters from my mom and some of my last letters from my father. His beautiful penmanship soothed my soul and put a huge smile on my face. The pressure on me to persevere grew day by day. I was not only representing myself, but I was also representing The Conteh Family name.

As I continued training, the leader in me was slowly being formed, the seeds of leadership were taking root. I wanted my family to be proud that their Adama was a military woman. My father was the proudest and always boasted of my military status to relatives, although he always mistakenly told them I was in the Army. I was not fortunate enough to have my family at my basic training graduation; I knew our situation. But one thing for sure, my family was always in my heart, no matter where my journey led me in life.

My faith in God was my peace of mind and constant companion. I made a lot of great friends during basic training; some I know are doing well in their various careers. I was a member of Flight #321 platoon and will carry the Air

Force values for life: "Integrity first, service before self, and excellence in all we do." I have carried these values with me beyond the Air Force, into my local community and outreach. We all built bonds and developed what many lack, the ability to work with people of all backgrounds to meet a common goal. For anyone who is deployed on the battlefield, when you are at war, the enemy sees no color, so working as a team is critical. My training was followed by technical school at Sheppard Air Force Base where I began a career in dietary services. It is here that I developed a deep passion for public health and wellness.

    The loss of my father made it so difficult to sleep at night; I kept the lights on throughout. I had very little friends so travelling by public transportation to go to my family's house in DC was my soothing comfort. I took many walks on the base with tears rolling down my eyes and a heart aching in pain, mainly because I didn't feel my dad had seen me reach the height of success he always dreamed of. I don't think you truly heal from losing a parent. You simply find the courage to face each day without them while imagining they are there. After several long months of depression, trying to find joy from meaningless influences, I was fortunate to find God again and rededicate my life to Him. Though the journey was not easy, it was the survival kit I needed to face the storms in life. I saw that though I suffered loss, I gained a stronger faith in God and a belief that greater things were coming for Adama. In that moment, I decided it was time to improve myself in all areas. I finally got braces to correct my overbite and crooked teeth. As corny as it may seem, getting braces changed my life for the better. Not saying that having straight teeth makes one beautiful, but it enhanced the beauty that was already within me and boosted my confidence. I also decided to further my education. My military career supported my dream to go to college and expand my knowledge. Starting my educational journey at the Community College of the Air Force was both rewarding and challenging, as I attended classes after my workday. The Air Force Community College was my first step into higher education and gave me the core essentials to be a great student. There was one course in particular, a mandatory course I tried to avoid called, Public Speaking 101.

Although I now have what appears to be a bubbly personality, I am naturally shy and an introvert. I still carried deep insecurities and wanted to avoid speaking at all costs. But as I mentioned, this was a mandatory course and there was no escaping it. I had to meet my fate. Surprisingly, it was not the nightmare I thought. Rather, I found that my voice mattered.

One of my presentations was on teenage pregnancy and I took the class back to a familiar song by Tupak Shakur called, "Brenda's Got a Baby". I presented a different view on teenage pregnancy providing insight that really impressed my professor. Eventually, I earned enough college credits to attend the University of the District of Columbia (UDC) in pursuit of a public health degree. The college exposure made me more comfortable in myself as I began realizing that so many people have insecurities. Education is the best solution for ignorance and intolerance. I developed a deep passion for my education and saw I had a deep love for writing. I also loved to engage with others and learned the value of networking. This was recognized by many of my professors, and it gave me a lot of confidence. Eventually, this combination along with my positive nature led to many other doors opening. I found value in developing deep connections with my peers and faculty and soon became involved with many organizations. I joined the Student Government and served as the volunteer coordinator for campus activities. The seed of community service was truly born during this time. I was awarded a scholarship from the Thurgood Marshall Scholarship Fund (TMSF) which helped me fully pay for my college education. I was so honored to receive such an award named after one of our most memorable figures of the Civil Rights Movement, the Honorable Thurgood Marshall. This was an incredible experience that helped carve my character and train me for the working world. The invaluable mentorship provided by the TMSF helped shape the person I have become to this day. This led to another open door: I was chosen to be an AmeriCorps fellow under the Corporation for National Service. This opportunity, which was similar to the American version of Peace Corps, an initiative started by former President John F. Kennedy, paid an additional stipend that helped pay for school. I served as a Volunteer Coordinator and was then hired by the organization as Volunteer Director who supervised incoming AmeriCorps fellows. I learned so many valuable leadership tools while in this role and started to see a glimpse of where I would thrive most in the world – service.

These accomplishments all had a common theme – community service. I found that many doors of opportunities opened once I embraced serving. My service in the United States Air Force transformed into a love for serving Africa. My seeds of service began in the military, continued in college, and eventually grew into a lifetime of serving others. The ugly experiences I endured as a child built my character and developed me into a strong woman. Going into the military helped me to rediscover the strong, resilient woman within me and pushed me to improve myself in every way possible. The ugly duckling has indeed become a swan who loves life. As I reflect on my life's journey, I realize that discovering my strength is the reason I use my voice to roar with confidence at every chance. With this same attitude, I now pour into others so that they too can find their voice to propel themselves into their greatest destinies.

Travel to Sierra Leone

My father and I had a special bond like no other and whenever he saw me, his eyes lit up and danced; and we shared a passion and love for Sierra Leone. His death ignited within me a desire to help our country with development as an obligation to keep his memory alive and continue his legacy through service. Making both of my parents proud as I help Sierra Leone is a big motivation. It is said that the eyes are the windows to the heart. My heart is full of love and compassion for those suffering from lack of necessities.

My first visit to Sierra Leone was on a cold, winter day in December 2003. I was flying out of Dulles International Airport and upon my arrival handed my travel documents over and checked in for boarding. I was travelling under a popular last name: Conteh, which was my father's name, and was in disbelief that I was finally travelling to Mama Africa, the land of my parents and those who came before them. Just a week prior, my previously planned flight was cancelled unexpectedly but, somehow, I knew I would be going because this was my time, the beginning of a lifelong journey of purpose. Despite my reservations of not speaking the language fluently, my heart was filled with excitement, and I knew that all things would work together for my good.

Stepping off the plane, as I walked toward Lungi Airport, I felt the warmest sun kiss my face. I felt fearful and thrilled at the same time. But my worries were put at bay once I got past security and was met with a big sign that said, "Welcome Adama Conteh". I was welcomed with claps and cheers from my aunts and uncles in the waiting area. I felt so special at that moment because I knew I was finally home.

Touching the soil of Africa changed my life. I visited many relatives and each of them presented me with a gift of some sort. This is how they welcome visitors. Everyone was eager to feed me some delicious authentic cuisine: groundnut soup, fry stew and plantains, jollof rice, cassava leaves and my all-time favorite, potato leaves soup.

I was enthralled by the country and its natural beauty. The sunrise and sunset were magical. As we traveled through Freetown, I was amazed at how festive the place was at night. I had chosen the best time to visit, during the Christmas holiday in December. I was not fortunate enough to meet any of my grandparents alive but pleaded with family members to ensure I visited the gravesites of both my maternal and paternal grandparents, so we went. The grave sites for my paternal grandmother and great-grandmother were unforgettable.

They sat in front of a home my father had built in Yonibana. At each gravesite, we said special prayers and were offered kola nuts and water. Although I am Christian, I did not hesitate joining hands in prayer with my Muslim family.

Visiting my maternal grandmother's village Ro'Konta made me feel especially proud to bear her name. The village chiefs and elders welcomed me and, again, prayers were offered. In addition to being fed, I was gifted with chickens which is a typical gift to strangers from people living in rural areas. One moment that touched my heart was when I met my grandmother's siblings. They all wept when they saw me and said I looked a lot like their sister. They shared beautiful stories about how my grandmother was a great member of the community and was remembered for making gara fabrics and growing cassava. On the way to her village, we passed a vast forest land where I was told my grandparents once grew cocoa beans and coffee beans.

I visited more than six villages including Yonibana, my father's birthplace, and Ro' Konta, the birth home of my mother. The ride there was bumpy and dusty, but reaching my destination was priceless. I was welcomed by family and community members who had been anticipating my arrival. "James Conteh's daughter is coming here from America", they were told. When they laid eyes on me, they could see my father through me, and they instantly burst into tears. One aunt said warmly: "Wow you have your father's eyes. It's like your father has returned." I will always cherish this reminder that, through me, my father lives.

My father was a prominent figure in his village before his travels to America. The home he built was bombed by rebels during the 10-year civil war, but the structure was still standing. Seeing the devastation from the war was a sight I will never ever forget. It opened my eyes to how much I took for granted such as regular electricity and access to fresh clean drinking water. Each person I had met reminded me not to forget them and to do all that I could to help my people. Those words echoed in my mind as I returned to the States.

PICTURE OF A HOUSE IN YONIBANA WHICH WAS BOMBED BY THE REBELS

My visit was also bittersweet as I witnessed a beautiful country that has suffered too many pains over the years leading to a struggling economy. I vowed to myself that I would not allow society to classify Sierra Leone as a doomed country and decided to share the greatness of my country with the world. I instantly realized that as a daughter of Sierra Leone, I have a responsibility to use my American ties to advance the causes of the Motherland. I knew in my heart that any community service I was to do in the future would have to benefit Sierra Leone.

Since 2003, I've led several fundraising efforts to support local and rural communities in Sierra Leone.

Realizing there was so much more to do to help, I have completely embraced my true purpose which was to empower Sierra Leone. I traveled there each year, consecutively, from 2003 to 2006. I also traveled there from 2020 to 2024. My visits enhanced my strong desire and interest in using my knowledge, skills, and influence to advocate for the vulnerable. My life completely changed and has never been the same.

I now consider myself a major influencer of Sierra Leone as a Diasporan. For several years, I've made positive contributions to promote its culture, using photos to share my story, culture, and the beauty of my people with the world via several social media outlets. As an African American woman who was born to African parents, I have a great advantage and can serve as a bridge to connect both cultures, and I feel a sense of pride when I share my culture with my American friends. I also created two Facebook pages, "I Love Sierra Leone" and "Impact Sierra Leone", to share the culture and beauty of Sierra Leone. I have posted videos and pictures of Sierra Leone as well as featured cultural topics. I've used my love for African dance to create and post videos displaying cultural dances of Sierra Leone, sparking unity and pride among fellow Sierra Leoneans all over the world. Additionally, in my quest to learn Temne, the native tongue of my family members, I used books to translate and illustrate Temne phrases and posted them on social media. My family is from the Themne tribe, so this really made them proud. I've also endeavored to share the stories of my Sierra Leone family, especially my grandparents, whom I was not fortunate to meet. I would usually categorize these stories under the title: "Chronicles of the Diaspora Queen". Additionally, my commanding personality has made me a natural for hosting a series of successful fund-raising events through collaboration with community organizations and church groups in the Washington, D.C. area from 2004 through 2019. My social media posts have gained wide readership from Sierra Leoneans around the world and Americans who now have a deeper appreciation for Sierra Leone cultural values.

When I embraced my culture and heritage, my purpose became my power!

Because of my travels, my life changed for the better. I embraced two truths: black is beautiful and being from Africa is an honor. I began to stand tall with no shame when people marveled at my smooth, black complexion. As a daughter of Sierra Leone, I have a responsibility to use my American ties to advance the causes of The Motherland.

Seeds of History

I am delighted to know my history and roots. Although I did not always appreciate my African roots for various reasons as a child, over the years I've matured and have learned that knowing your history can help aid you in living a successful life.

Sierra Leone, while having its imperfections, is rich in history and cultural traditions. It is known for its early achievements in the fields of medicine, law, and education. These breakthrough foundations made it easier for me to keep up with all I am doing now, all my achievements and not just pen on paper. I'm always proud to know that Sierra Leone was known as the "Athens of West Africa." Fourah Bay College (University of Sierra Leone) was established in 1827 and produced some of the brightest scholars. I stand on the shoulders of many great men and women of Sierra Leone, whose accomplishments remind me that I am a queen in every way with the power to do great things!

In addition to the history of Sierra Leone, I have a huge appreciation for the history of my family. Over the years and through many hours of research, asking relatives questions, and listening to storytelling of elders, I have learned other personal historical facts of my own family. Although I never met any of them alive, I learned my grandparents were all entrepreneurs, leaders, all successful in farming, agriculture, and business. I am honored to share pieces of my family history which has influenced the woman I have become today.

My maternal grandmother, Ya Adama Kamara, was a giver in her hometown of Ro'Konta and highly respected. She was a successful farmer growing cassava and peanuts.

She was known for selling roasted peanuts around the village. I not only inherited her name, but also her beautiful cheek bones.

My paternal grandfather, Pa Saidu Conteh, was a successful businessman and prominent elder in the Yonibana community. He was born at Rochen Kamandao which is a town not very far from Masengbe in Sierra Leone. He was a general merchant dealing mainly in agricultural products like palm kernel nuts, ginger, tobacco, fabrics etc. I was blessed to meet his family in Yoni including his elder brother Idrisa Conteh. His gardens still grow cocoa beans!

My maternal grandfather, Pa Alhaji Musa Sesay, was a generous, successful businessman who loved to provide for his family. He was born in Rokel and raised in Mankobo, Tonkilili District in Yonibana, SL. His name, Musa, is the Muslim version of Moses which means leader. Indeed, he was the leader of the family. He worked hard mining diamonds and brought his three brothers along so that they could also be successful in Kono. He even has a street named after him in Kono District, Tongoman. I will certainly continue his legacy as his proud granddaughter.

My paternal grandmother, Ya Fatu Koroma, was a native of Yonibana and an entrepreneur who did all she could so that her family would not suffer from poverty. She was a petty trader and a businesswoman, but most importantly, she was a leader. She specialized in designing Gara and tie dye fabric designs and was known all over the village for this craft. Her skills in making these beautiful Gara fabrics was very successful and allowed her to build a house and enroll her children into very good schools. She was very creative with her Gara designs, creating different beautiful patterns like clouds and water on white fabric. In addition, she taught the younger girls in the family how to design Gara so that the skill would be passed onto the younger generation. She also made homemade peppermint candies and was a very hard-working farmer. She grew many different crops such as cassava, potatoes, and several herbs. In fact, she was known as an herbalist in the village and treated many people with medicinal leaves. I even learned other entrepreneurial talents my grandmother possessed – she made homemade soap out of caustic soda that was used for bathing and washing clothes. As a businesswoman and trader, she often travelled with her goods to other cities in Sierra Leone to sell and in turn brought other goods back to Yonibana to sell within the community. She bore four children, my father James Conteh aka "O Minnah" being her third born child.

Pa Katta Sesay is the first cousin of my maternal grandfather, Pa Alhaji Musa Sesay. When I visited the village of Rokel, he gathered the whole community to come and meet me, the stranger from the USA. He is one of the few educated, second-generation born of the Sesays. He was articulate, charming, and had a towering figure. After high school in the early sixties, he joined politics and contested to become a member of parliament for the Masimra Chief which covers Rokel, his place of birth. He lost the election to one other person from Lunsar. When the APC was overthrown in the early 1990s, multiple parties were reinstituted, and Pa Katta joined the newly former UNPP of the late political doyen, the Honorable, John Karefa Smart. Pa Katta later became a member of parliament until his death. He was known as a great and sound leader with the gift of storytelling.

    Although these family members have passed on, it is always an honor to keep their legacy alive through my humanitarian work. I stand on the shoulders of many great men and women of the past. The achievements and foundations of my forefathers are so critical to the work I am doing with Impact Sierra Leone. Education, medicine, and law are essential to our mission of reducing the country's socioeconomic challenges. These foundations also inspire us to raise future leaders in those fields. It is so important to embrace our history so that our stories are preserved and don't get lost! Our voices matter and need to be passed down to future generations.

The Journey of Impact

After many years of serving nonprofit groups and losing my job, I had considered several career options to include creative designer, wedding planner, floral designer, etc. Although these areas allowed me to use my heart's passion, they didn't seem like the best for my family and didn't generate enough income to pay the bills. In 2019 I decided that it was time to leap out on my own so I could serve in a greater capacity, thus, Impact Sierra Leone was born.

    Living in the United States has its advantages when it comes to access to quality education and other resources. We are privileged to have a strong middle class with many opportunities to become entrepreneurs with striving businesses. Growing up, I was privileged to have access to necessities that many all over the world greatly lack. In addition, the healthcare system is more robust in America than those in Africa which has contributed to my total wellness in performing my best. Being born in the United States provided me far more opportunities to succeed as a woman of color, but my African roots have shaped me to become a global servant leader.

Sierra Leone is a beautiful country with great potential that has suffered much over the years. My visit there helped me to realize the tremendous need to help rebuild a fragile nation which still harbors the trappings of instability. I observed many of the disparities in the economy, education and health systems, and the vast amount of poverty within the country.

Witnessing these disparities firsthand increased my passion for helping others and my devotion to the service of humanity was crystallized.

My advice to children who are first-generation born Americans is to love your culture enough to want to help improve your country. For those Sierra Leone descendants, we must unite as one so we can restore it to its former glory. My hope is that my mission will inspire other descendants of Africa to embrace their culture and positively impact their home country. I have a responsibility to be a voice, to raise my voice and to inspire others to help the causes in Africa. As descendants, we serve as a bridge and connection between our United States culture and our African culture. Our current program called the Seeds of Life allows us to reach students and provide them with a solid foundation to help them reach their greatest potential.

Our outreach brings hope to people who are living in impoverished conditions. As founder of this organization, I've been able to work with great people to serve orphans, farmers, students, women, and young girls. Engaging in these communities has had its triumphs and challenges, but it has helped me grow in so many areas. My heart is full each time farmers harvest crops and the other monthly empowerment activities.

Our organization has contributed meaningfully to the fields of education and health for girls and women in my ancestral village. There are far less opportunities for women as compared to men. I saw firsthand when I visited rural villages in Sierra Leone that many of the women are silenced and limited to domestic work. I've joined in the fight against injustices, stereotypes, discrimination, and inhumanity due to gender by promoting empowerment programs. By empowering other women to have a voice, we are impacting future generation of leaders who will ensure a world of inclusiveness and equality where all are valued. I strive to promote gender equality in all our projects. Our Seeds of Life Program includes a special Women's Farm project that engages women in growing crops while learning skills. This project has now become the Women's Agribusiness Collective which comprises of forty women farmers that we support with seeds, farm supplies and learning materials. I stand proud to give voice to women and girls and empower them through skills training and mentorship. I feel proud to be a voice and advocate for women and children in Sierra Leone. I chose, as primary focus, to help support women and girls in rural areas because of their huge lack of resources and access to services. The chains of gender bias must be broken in every facet of life from the medical field, political arena, business industry, and professional careers. This must occur globally. There needs to be a total mindset shift to eradicate the notion that women are inferior.

Men could contribute to women's empowerment by changing their mindset and ensuring that at their homes, workplaces, businesses, the women around them are afforded opportunities to succeed. Men should provide a safe place for the women in their circles and be a catalyst for change. Women's equality will be the driving force towards more positive change in the world. The poet Maya Angelou penned a powerful poem titled, "Phenomenal Woman" and indeed this is true. The fight for women inclusion must never end and needs to be championed by every citizen. Men in key leadership roles should ensure their female counterparts are included in the decision-making process. Breaking the bias must happen at every level from the executive office to the most remote village in rural West Africa. We need more awareness, resources and policies set in place and this can be done via training workshops, women's equality groups, social media platforms and within the workplace. Much like how we won the war on slavery and overcame many setbacks from the Civil Rights Movement, we can win the war on Women's Inequality and do it Together. Women Leadership must be a priority especially for all women of color! Let us stand up, raise our voices, act, and join forces to erase gender inequality worldwide. Additionally, I have a responsibility as a daughter of Africa to use my American ties to advance the causes of the motherland.

I hope to collaborate with other Civil Society Organizations (CSOs) and International Development Partners to empower women and take Sierra Leone to the next level. I endeavor to promote female empowerment throughout Sierra Leone. Our main motto is: "United We Stand and Together We Rise to Make a Difference!" I hope that my efforts will inspire other descendants of Africa to embrace their culture and positively impact their home country.

I never dreamed of leading my own foundation, I simply just wanted to help people improve their lives. I cannot take credit for our organization's success alone as so many others have sacrificed their time, money, and energy to see us succeed. Due to our success, we have been honored to receive many awards and accolades. I am also forever grateful to every soul who has given in one way or the other to our organization. It means the world to me to be able unite people around a great cause. Impact Sierra Leone is a humanitarian movement not just for our present time but for future generations to come. I hope to leave a legacy for my two children, Jonathan and Miriam.

There is power in our voices, power in our stories and power in our togetherness. I look forward to continuing my journey to alleviate poverty among people in need and making strides within the business ecosystem for Africa and the global good.

I truly believe the many seeds planted in me such as compassion, empathy, and goodwill have created a lasting harvest that will transform lives for years to come. I hope to make an impact on other leaders across the globe, those who share the Diaspora dream. As a Diasporan, I have an incredible power to affect change through my connections. I am empowered to inspire, and the best is yet to come!

Voices of Impact

I am Bold, Brave, Blessed, Beautiful, and Brilliant is one of the many affirmations I use to start my mornings powerfully! If you have not yet realized, what we say to ourselves can determine our future path. But for many, overwhelming life challenges can make it so hard to think positively. Imagine eating only once a day, surrounded by hardship, constant sickness, dependent on what is grown on the farm to eat, no access to a public restroom or clean drinking water. This is the harsh reality for some of the vulnerable populations we work with currently from rural farming communities. Yet, on my travels, I've met some remarkable individuals who manage to stay positive and inspirational. They allow their voices to be heard, advocating for themselves and their communities despite their circumstances.

The Voice of Change

I take you on a journey to the remote village of Foindu, located in rural Sierra Leone, West Africa where the hardships I just mentioned is a stark reality. My Uncle introduced me to this farming community in 2020 after I expressed a desire to support a village that was not receiving any support that had a great need for basic resources. I also expressed my interest in farming because both of my parents grew up with farmers in their families. My uncle described this as a place people normally don't come and visit because of its location. There are no tourist attractions, just a community of very hard-working farmers who are unfortunately just surviving and not thriving. It has become my heart's passion to help them thrive and to be their advocate.

Memories of my first visit to Foindu are still in my head. The bumpy ride on the rich red dirt as African music played on the radio brought me a huge smile. On the way to the village, I enjoyed sweet plantains and stew prepared by members of my team to ensure I didn't reach the village on an empty stomach. As our vehicle passed through to reach the village, we would see onlookers stop and gaze for they knew someone important is in that vehicle, well so I thought to myself anyway. I did feel like a celebrity as the people waved and some even clapped as we drove by, perhaps because they did not often see big cars in their village. As much as I wanted to feel the country air, the dust was a bit much, so I adhered to my team's advice to keep the window up as we drove.

When we finally reached our destination, many people had already assembled in the square as if they had been fully informed of my visit. I was met with clapping and a welcome song. Upon arrival, I was instantly drawn to the people, most of whom were farmers with children. With their eyes filled with hope, they received me with open arms. My Uncle introduced me in a way fitting of a government official and at first, I was a bit intimidated. Why? ... I only considered myself a normal person whose maternal roots were somehow connected to Foindu. After the introduction, I was given the chance to speak with my uncle as my interpreter wearing my Brand Impact Sierra Leone t-shirt. Even though I spoke English, they all cheered when I stated, I am here to help Foindu with better education and support for the farmers This first meet and greet to Foindu concluded with clothes and shoes giveaway with a delicious plate of my favorite, Potato Leaves soup. I was just excited to learn more about my roots and this ignited me to visit them and be a support in any way I can. Not just for me, but for the grandmother I never met alive whose voice I represented. I was not only desiring to be a voice, I wanted to be a voice for all my ancestors, a voice of transformation, a voice of victory. I made a vow to myself that even as a single woman, I would do all I can to improve their current situation.

I learned from my uncle that day that most of the farmers were not literate, unable to read and write. But, seeing their smiles and hearing their voices of joy that day was a huge motivation for me to return to America with a solid plan of support.

Fast forward, a few years of supporting their farming activities and figuring out the best path forward at Foindu, we eventually created our anchor program, the Seeds of Life, which allows us to reduce poverty in the greatest capacity. Creating this program made it easier to promote the Sustainable Development Goals (SDG's) reaching wider audiences. This program also reminded me how important it is to be creative with the communities you serve and to include them in your outreach, so their voices are heard. As a child, I loved art and creating artistic designs on paper. I decided a great way to empower this community was using my gifts and talents to create empowerment posters. Not only was it a good way to promote reading, but it was also a way to educate them on wellness and nutrition.

One of the many ways I enjoy helping others find their voice is by making empowerment visual posters. I remember one day I was faced with so much uncertainty about how I can best make an impact. I have always known that the voice within each of us has power to lead us higher. One truth that rings true is that you cannot help others discover their voice and their true self if you have not discovered your own voice. The moment I discovered my voice and my power; I felt a strong sense to help others find their voice so they too can be an inspiration in the world. It has been an honor being a voice of change for others and speaking for others who may have been silenced and didn't feel their voice mattered for one reason or the other.

In these next chapters, I will highlight some unique and amazing people whose voices as well as their stories impacted my journey. Enjoy these voices representing the girl child, the youth, the farmer, the woman, and the NGO leader.

The Voice of Humanity - Adamsay

I take you to the amazing young girl who shares my name, Adama aka Adamsay. She is a girl child attending the school from our partner community in Foindu Village. The first time I saw her was in videos shared with me by the project coordinator as the children enjoyed planting crops in their school garden through our efforts. While all the children were amazing, Adamsay stood out in a special way, and I was quite inspired by her voice and smile. Given the disparaging statistics and grim surroundings, I often wondered if children lacking basic resources could even find reason to smile. Were their fears the same as others around the world … Finally, the day came when I would meet these amazing children in person, it was almost like a reunion.

Not knowing her name, the first thing I noticed about Adamsay were her features, beautiful ebony skin, warm smile, almond eyes, and model-like physique. Not only that, but she was also very intelligent and spoke with such poise. This was a characteristic I noticed while listening to her read a book we shipped from our book drive. She stood confidently amongst her peers with her white uniform shirt, and I was quite impressed. She reminded me of my younger self in a way. What she also represented was an African girl child, one of the most vulnerable populations.

Now I love all children, but I've always had a soft spot in my heart for the young girls, knowing their plight, especially those growing up in the village was marked with limitations due to childhood marriage, early teenage pregnancy, child labor and female genital mutilation. Statistics show that many of these girls do not complete their primary education and fewer enroll in junior secondary education. My drive and passion for girls' empowerment inspires me to be their voice and help them realize their worth. My dream for Adamsay and all the beautiful children is to grow healthy, finish school, go to college and then become a change agent who gives back to the world. I want them to become great people in their society by also giving back to their home, Sierra Leone.

My second visit to Foindu was very special because it came after a year of supporting and engaging with the children and families all year round. Our first effort was helping the children start a school farm, planting permanent crops. The children learned about the benefits of the crops through the visual posters I created. I still remember walking through the village town being greeted by everyone as the visitor from the West. Then I stumbled by women and girls gathered in what I felt was a special activity. I quickly told my people, take me to where they are because their joyful faces are drawing my spirit. The women and girls were preparing the afternoon meal by pounding rice in a wooden bowl, not just any bowl, it was one that was mighty and strong.

I was amazed at seeing these women and girls of various ages pound the rice with such strength. The beautiful thing was hearing them talk in their native tongue. I didn't understand all they were saying but felt in my heart. After gazing in amazement for some time, I decided I must experience this for myself and pull out my own strength. I asked them if I could try ... they all happily agreed and even cheered me on as I pounded the stick up and down. From afar, it seemed like an effortless activity but after few rhythmic pounds, I discovered, the stick was heavy and pounding rice was no easy task, especially judging by the muscles on all the women. I then began to join in their dialect, well at least I tried. It was a good feeling to see their excitement as I joined in on their cultural activity. I watched Adamsay pound the rice with such ease which led me to realize this is a daily activity for them. I made sure to encourage the girls and reminded them that they were beautiful and amazing! The girls joined me in rhythmic dances after we pounded the rice which we captured in priceless photos and videos.

As a young African American woman who is a descendent of Sierra Leone, I always feel a strong urge to encourage the young girls, especially those in Sierra Leone. The young girls inspired me to design an empowerment poster: *"I am Bold, Brave, Beautiful, & Brilliant."* I am always moved by the young girls because if my mom never traveled to the US, I would be this girl in Sierra Leone. Empowering women and young girls can truly change communities in a great way. I also recognize in many parts of West Africa; women's rights are overshadowed by cultural traditions. Due to my experience of volunteerism, I've felt a great sense of responsibility and inspiration to become an Ambassador and Agent-of-change for young girls and women in Sierra Leone. Female Empowerment inspires a whole generation of female leaders, what we truly need to make Sierra Leone greater. My visit to the village reminded me why women and girls empowerment is one of our key areas of focus within my missionary work… women and girls in rural areas suffer more because of their huge lack of resources and access to services. They have higher chances of experiencing early child marriage, child abuse, teenage pregnancy, female genital mutilation, child rape and child labor. Instead of these grim outcomes, I desire to expose them to African Dance, Quality Education, Arts/Crafts, Singing, Drama, Stem/Science, etc.

    My message for the girl child and women who may not be where they are is to never, ever give up on your dreams and goals. If you believe in yourself and have a good heart, there is so much good you can do in the world. I would remind them that they are the following: Bold, Beautiful, Brilliant and Brave. I would also remind them that they should bloom where they are planted. I would advise them to search their heart for their true purpose. Discover what truly makes you happy. Search for a cause that does not seem like work but drives your passion daily. My other advice would be to serve without expectations – the reward is in seeing the needs of the people you are serving met. Most importantly, it is to build great friendships with those who serve with you. Great relationships mean great service! One should take things step by step to reach your greatest potential in life. We all have greatness within us and the capacity to succeed beyond our imaginations. To all the beautiful women and girls in Sierra Leone, I remind you that you are capable of being great changemakers in your community and inspiring leaders.

I join with others in prioritizing children's rights, especially the rights of the girlchild:

- ✓ Every girlchild deserves the right to a good education.
- ✓ Every girlchild deserves the right to be Safe.
- ✓ Every girlchild deserves the right to be loved and not used as a bargaining chip.
- ✓ Every girlchild deserves the right to be protected from child trafficking, child labor, child abuse.

The Voice of Talent - Alfred

One of the joys I experienced while visiting Africa is being surrounded by the children and how eager they were to see this stranger visit their village. I remember meeting Alfred, one of the outspoken youths I saw through videos shared with me by the coordinators. I knew instantly he was ambitious and a leader. He was perhaps between the ages of 12 and 14, dark skinned with a huge smile. He also appeared to have a sense of humor as he engaged with the other students on video. I first met Alfred in person performing an African cultural dance during a Christmas event in 2022. It was quite impressive. He danced with such confidence and truly made me proud. His team won the dance competition. He then competed in the Spelling Bee competition and was also the winner. I knew then he was exceptional and stood out among his peers. During this same visit, I visited the farms, trekking on foot for a considerable distance. Some of the children followed us to the farm with Alfred included. At some point at the farm, I connected with the children by simply asking them about their experience with the farm and school. While most of the children were shy, Alfred stood out as a leader and stated the farming projects are good for the community. He shared that the one thing they needed more was support for the youth to play soccer because this was very important for empowerment. Alfred stated he plays football very well but that their village never had a soccer team, due to lack of funding and supplies. I took his request to heart because I always believed the adage, "You do not have because you do not ask". I told Alfred because you have voiced this need, I will see what I can do to assist, and his eyes smiled. I then took the time to quickly ask the children, "So what do you guys want to be when you grow older"? Most stated they wanted to be a teacher, a lawyer, a nurse but Alfred boldly stated he wanted to be an artist. It was right then the light went off in my head and I recalled a young man at Foindu I was told draws very well and loves art. I asked Alfred immediately, were you the student that entered your drawing for a competition we participated in with a Child Safety organization group? He instantly replied with a smile, "Yes Aunty, it was me who drew the pictures." I reminded him that he was extremely talented and had potential to do great things. At that moment, I believe that Alfred felt a push to work harder because I told him that he would do great things. This moment was somewhat nostalgic; Alfred represented more than himself. He represented young boys in Africa who were often left out and not heard. He represented the young boys who fell victim to being recruited as child soldiers during the ten-year civil war Siera Leone endured. He represented talented youth who just lacked opportunity and finances to reach their greatest potential. He also told stories of many young people living in impoverished communities. Some had never celebrated a special occasion, especially a birthday. On a more personal note, he reminded me of my younger brother Musa who fell into the wrong crowd at the wrong time and passed away in 2020 with so much talent and potential. Musa is a driving force for me to always remember the young boys and to be their voice of encouragement. I continue to see him in all the little boys I meet, and his spirit pushes me to fight their cause and create pathways for their success. For Alfred, perhaps my voice was the push he needs to pursue a career in art and who knows, we just might have a future Picasso from Sierra Leone take over the world of art. His talent will not just be limited to the village of Foindu or even in Sierra Leone but will cross borders. I highly encourage us all to seek ways to become mentors to our future generation because they really need our advocacy and our voice. Just think perhaps my voice and the right tools, can propel Alfred to his greatest Destiny and a victorious journey.

The Voice of Power - Huldah Imah Paul

I am honored to share about an exceptional young lady who served as Impact Sierra Leone's Finance Manager and a lifelong Female Empowerment leader, Ms. Huldah Imah-Paul. She is in my book, ten women in one body and is a powerful force. Born in Sierra Leone but raised in the Gambia and Nigeria, Huldah is the second of three girls born to her parents. She hails from a very respectable home where values of integrity, service and compassion were instilled at an early age. Huldah's voice and the power of her voice makes her stand out from many of her peers. I consider this remarkable young lady to be a Triple "E" Queen: *educated, empowered,* and *equipped* to do mighty things.

I would describe Huldah in five ways: dedicated to the mission, resourceful, social justice advocate, organized, and God fearing beyond measure. She is a woman of character and outstanding values. She is indeed a voice for the voiceless, for vulnerable children, especially the young girl children, or young mothers, and for the homeless. I have personally witnessed her humanity in action and giving heart. What sets Huldah apart is how she embodies wisdom, strength, and sacrifice for others at such a young age. She was cut from a different cloth having earned her diploma in Mechanical Engineering, a career that was questioned by her peers, but Huldah being resilient stayed true to her pursuit despite any naysayers.

Huldah shared her favorite quote with me, "I learn to give not because I have much, but because I know exactly how it feels to have nothing" by Mavic Cruz. Her humility and dedication to helping others has always impressed me in a great way. I first met Huldah in 2020 through a mutual contact as we were collaborating on how to bring light to orphans in need. Huldah was literally the first volunteer of Impact Sierra Leone in Africa and has served me in the greatest capacity. She has been our voice on the ground in Sierra Leone and was responsible for bringing on many of the volunteers with our organization today. When I see Huldah, I see a Nation Builder, Capacity Builder and a true woman of power with a heart of gold.

When asked about a time where she used her voice to impact, Huldah shared how she helped a young woman who hit rock bottom, almost to the point of taking her life, by simply being her listening ear and pouring positivity and as a result, this young lady was able to rebuild herself again and is thriving today. Huldah wears many different hats; and while it is not always easy, she maintains a positive mindset, never complaining but finding the best ways to get the job done. She is an advisor, an advocate, a mentor, a female empowerment leader, and a visionary.

Huldah has used her voice to advance the mission of so many charitable organizations around the globe to include Smiling Through Light, Impact Sierra Leone, Women Ascension, Community Hands Organization, Second Chance Fashions and more. What's even more amazing is that her dedication to empowering vulnerable children, especially girls in Sierra Leone led her to launch her own organization called Defend You. The mission of this organization is: To defend the youth, orphans and underprivileged children and eradicate vulnerability in society. She currently provides safe housing, education, daily feeding, empowerment and enrichment activities, helping these girls grow into healthy and responsible young ladies. Huldah, at such a young age, has become their mother and provides them with abundant love. I was privileged to visit this home last year and was so impressed by how the girls were well taken care of despite very little resources. I enjoyed taking a tour of their home and even visited their garden where they were growing cassava leaves, potato leaves and other nutritious crops which they used in making authentic delicious soup. It was very impressive to see the girls learning about the power of agriculture at such a young age. During this special visit, Huldah and I collaborated to empower the girls through poetry reading. I truly enjoyed quality time with Huldah and the girls, asking them what they hoped to be when they were older. It was beautiful to hear their future aspirations such as a caterer, nurse, doctor, lawyer, artist and more. Huldah shares my vision of ensuring our children we support feel heard and respected. I am confident that under Huldah's leadership and passion, Defend You organization will grow and make a lasting impact in Sierra Leone. Huldah used this same inherited passion at Impact Sierra Leone and for that she always makes me a proud CEO.

There is a quote that says, "Coming together is the beginning, staying together is the progress, working together is success." Indeed, this is true because Impact Sierra Leone would not be where it is today without Huldah's guidance and leadership. Impact Sierra Leone currently serves communities in the northern region of Foindu Village as well as Freetown. Huldah has led several of our wellness workshops, Child Safety workshops, Literacy Drives, Clothing Drives, Feeding Days, Annual Christmas outreach events and more. One of the most memorable ways Huldah has used her voice powerfully is during the Impact Sierra Leone Women's Empowerment Brunch held in March 2021 which was our celebration of International Women's Day. While I could not attend in person, Huldah executed the event to perfection following my guidance from the States. She joined cultural singing with forty women farmers and the community nurses. She represented me well taking many pictures and videos and ensuring the women felt empowered. The theme for that event was based on the United Nations "Break the Bias". Huldah's ability to wear many hats with such poise, precision and positivity is highly admirable.

In another memorable moment, I recall when Huldah and the Country Director traveled to Foindu Village to take part in the harvesting of 32 bags of ground nuts. Ther voyage to the farm was not easy, taking a canoe, trekking on foot and sitting with the farmers to hand pick the ground nuts. I will never forget this dedication to our sustainable development goals. Huldah ensured to motivate the farmers during this time as the workload was much but with determination, they accomplished the goal. This is just one of the many ways Huldah's efforts led to a victorious outcome!

She dedicates time each month in partnership with a Global partner purchasing fruits and vegetables for over 250 school children in the village. Huldah used her voice to tell our story, sharing each time about the journey of our impact through videos so that we keep our supporters informed. In addition, whenever I visit Sierra Leone, she goes above and beyond to make sure I am safe, and my needs are met so that I can be effective in my outreach. I won't hesitate to say that she has been my advocate on many occasions. When I think of someone whose voice has an impact on many, Huldah is one of the first to come to my mind. As a result of her excellence in humanitarian work, Huldah has received multiple awards and honors. She has participated in many cross-cultural and global events. Huldah always makes a way out of no way and if I could personalize her life motto, it would be the following, "Nothing is impossible! If you dedicate your mind towards a goal every day, you will find a way to make it happen! She continues to fight against inequalities, especially gender inequality in Africa. In Huldah's voice, there is strength, boldness, and inspiration. Huldah and I are very similar in our character and beliefs. We also share a passion for agriculture and seeds. We realize that we are all seeds in this world destined to blossom into beautiful flowers. If Huldah and I were to hold an Empowerment workshop for adolescent girls in Sierra Leone, I imagine we would give each girl a bag of seeds. Along with these seeds we would give them a yellow bag with a rose gold mirror, a writing journal/pen, a picture of a flower, a heart-shaped box that says, "You are beautiful.", scented oils and an extra special note of inspiration. On this note would be the following words: "Imagine yourself sitting in a garden. How do you visualize it to be? Full of colors, flowers and beauty. Let's make that garden a reality. Let's plant the seeds of these flowers in our mind first because things happen twice, once in our minds, then in the real world. Just like a gardener we have the power to nurture these seeds, to cultivate them into something beautiful.

Let's transform this garden into a big field of success!" You are a beautiful garden so don't be afraid to blossom. In this very moment, our victory would not be in our ability to have a great workshop, our victory would be from empowering these young ladies to discover their inner beauty, inner strength and potential to be victorious! I know without a doubt that Huldah's voice will reach many corners of the world as she continues to walk in greatness.

The Voice of Empowerment

I write this chapter in dedication to the women of Sierra Leone but most especially to the women farmers of Foindu Village in rural Sierra Leone. In 2022, my organization was privileged to launch the Women's Agribusiness Collective made up of forty women farmers from Foindu, a remote community in the Northern part of the country.

When I first met these women in 2021, they spoke very little and did not smile much. Their shyness was a mystery but did not stop me from trying to make them smile and I think they appreciated my efforts to bring them light. I recall the moment during this visit as I gathered around the people to take pictures and was mostly surrounded by the men and village leaders. After some time, I noticed the women gazing at me from afar, I quickly called them over with excitement to please come and join me in pictures. I can tell they felt a small sense of happiness from this act of inclusion. This was the beginning of our empowerment journey together. Forty women with a desire for a better life, with a determination to rise above their circumstances, with families they want to feed, all who have survived the tragic ten-year civil war that overshadowed Sierra Leone in 1991.

After this first encounter with the women, I was eager to return so that I can make a difference in their mindset. I recognized in that moment that life had somehow silenced them and made them think their voice did not matter. The cultures they were born into perhaps gave them no choice but to accept inferiority because of their gender. As a first generation born, I have insight on gender issues both in the United States and in West Africa. There seems to be a common factor between the two regions and that is there are far less opportunities for women as compared to men.

The playing field has yet to be leveled because we see too often that a woman's skills or experiences are considered less important than her gender. As a global leader, I join others in the fight against injustices, stereotypes, discrimination, and inhumanity due to gender by promoting empowerment programs. By empowering other women to have a voice, I can impact future generation of leaders who will ensure a world of inclusiveness and equality where all are valued. One of the best moments at the end of this visit was giving the women a mic to speak and share what they wanted to see in their community. I could see in their eyes that by giving them a mic to speak, I unknowingly put them at ease and gave them a sense of freedom. To paint a clear picture, as the women spoke in their native dialect, which was Temne, an interpreter translated what they were saying to me in English. It was sort of an impromptu language learning session that I will always cherish. The women all agreed that their biggest desire was to see a better school for their children. The women also shared a desire to have their very own farming project and to learn new skills. I was the last to speak that day and concluded by affirming that their voices were heard and that I would do my best to support their requests. I returned to America with so many thoughts but mostly my mind replayed their voices. I knew it was important that I did my best to support them with a farm project, but this would not happen overnight. This was a seed being planted that would eventually grow into something phenomenal.

In March 2022, I was so excited to coordinate a Women's Empowerment Meet and Greet for the women of Foindu on the heels of Women's History Month. The women again expressed the need to have their own farm project and to be change agents in the community. After hearing their voices again, I came up with the idea of forming the women into a group. With the help of village leaders and stakeholders, a sign up was initiated for any women interested in being in a farm group supported by Impact Sierra Leone. The goal would be to provide these women with seedlings to plant, training and eventually teach them a skill which could help them make additional income. We officially launched the Women's Farm Collaborative, which is now the Women's Agribusiness Collective, in April 2022 providing the women farmers with seeds, farming tools and fertilizer. They would grow common crops such as peanuts, okra, and peppers on their own plot of land to help feed their families. Since that time, the women have planted groundnuts, cassava, cucumbers, krain krain, peppers, and beans. It's amazing to see how the program has transformed these women from once being shy to now being joyful and smiling more. The women desire to grow many other crops to restore hope in the community and boost food production in Sierra Leone. I strongly believe that empowering women through agriculture and other social mobility initiatives will not only improve their lives but the lives of their children, spouses, and community. I also believe that the farming project will be a springboard for other female empowerment initiatives in Foindu that will reduce poverty and promote sustainable development.

Working with these women reminded me that the best way to achieve as women in this era is by using our voices! Being a voice for others, and helping others find their voice so they too can reach their best potential is paramount. I recently read a beautiful quote by Louisa May Alcott, "An Old-Fashioned Girl" and it reads, "The emerging woman ... will be strong-minded, strong-hearted, strong-souled, and strong-bodied ... strength and beauty must go together." This quote reminds me of these forty women who all have the potential to be leaders. I am highly honored because I get to help develop these women into courageous, compassionate, creative, charismatic, confident, capacity builders who will be catalysts of change.

The sadness that often comes to these women is due to the lack of basic resources and food scarcity. For this reason, I include morale building activities to keep them inspired such as workshops, feeding days, and from time to time, clothes donations. This is my way to show them I care about their wellbeing. I want these women to know they are role models and that everything we do not only affects us but our future generation. To be catalysts for positive change, we must begin with ourselves. We are uniquely designed for greatness ... there are no two persons alike. Our value-add stems from our unique shape, experiences, skill sets, and background. We all have something to bring to the table, and knowing what you bring to the table is key. If you don't know your value, then no one else will recognize your value or worth. We all have greatness within us and the capacity to succeed beyond our imaginations.

Most importantly, it is imperative to build great friendships with those who serve with you. Great relationships mean great service! One should take things step by step to reach your greatest potential in life. Simon T. Bailey once stated, "It's not who you are that holds you back from brilliant success, it's who you think you're not that holds you back"

The launch of this Farm Collaborative group also led us to develop an initiative under our anchor program, Seeds of Life, and that is called the Women and Girls Empowerment Initiative, also known as W.A.G.E. Women's equality will be the driving force to more positive change in the world. The fight for women's inclusion must never end and needs to be championed by every citizen. Breaking the bias must happen at every level from the executive office to the most remote village in rural West Africa. There remains a huge disparity around the world between the numbers of women in leadership positions compared to the number of male leaders. This disparity is even more discouraging when one takes into consideration that women make up half of the world's population. We need more awareness, resources and policies set in place and this can be done via training workshops, women's equality groups, social media platforms and within the workplace. Women Leadership must be a priority especially for all women of color!

Within the village of Foindu, women have less opportunities to be entrepreneurs compared to their male counterparts. However, all of them lack vocational skills. Our future goal with the Women's Farm Collaborative is to build a vocational training center where they can learn skills such as garment making and food processing. With the learned skills, they will be able to sell their goods in local and international markets and generate income for their families and community. We will also strengthen these women in agriculture techniques. As sustainable agriculture is becoming increasingly needed and a sought-after skill, farmers will learn new farming techniques and participate in live demonstrations to boost their farming success. Farmers will also join in virtual farm training with the Diaspora community. Women and girls can learn the fundamentals of garment making. The center will house sewing machines to be used for making clothes and materials to sell. They will be taught how to use sewing machines, sewing techniques using fabrics and incorporating the expertise of skilled seamstresses. Eventually, they will be able to use this skill to generate income for themselves and their families. Men can learn carpentry, shoe making, and auto mechanics, etc. which can also generate income.

With these women, my efforts are depositing dreams, motivating their daily lives, encouraging their souls, bringing peace to their minds, and giving them a sense of purpose as they cope with the hardships of daily life. To all the beautiful women and girls in Sierra Leone, I remind you that you are capable of being great changemakers in your community and inspiring leaders. I am so proud of the women and girls I've been fortunate to help within Impact Sierra Leone. I am essentially providing them with tools to succeed. Now their voices have been amplified, and it is a joy to hear them singing praise songs during the various farm activities. By investing in their wellbeing, I'm not only developing future womenpreneurs, but I am also igniting a movement and helping them walk in victory! To leave you with my favorite quote, "United We Stand, Together We Rise". Let us stand up, raise our voices, act, and join forces to erase gender inequality worldwide.

I AM Adama

Allow me to re-introduce myself. Today, I am Dr. Adama Kalokoh, a leader in women's empowerment, a worldwide humanitarian, chairperson of the Global Goodwill Ambassadors Foundation (GGAF), an advocate for the Sustainable Development Goals, and one of the Most Distinguished Women Change Makers in Africa for 2020–2021.

I am a successful African woman who is a change maker in a variety of professions and businesses. My enthusiasm for international development, public health, agriculture, and education inspired me to start my foundation as a proud descendant of Sierra Leone, West Africa, to better meet the needs of disadvantaged areas. I have been making a difference in people's lives in Sierra Leone for more than 20 years, starting with my first trip there in 2003.

Through various social media platforms, I have shared my narrative, my culture, and the beauty of my people with the world. As a Diasporan, I believe I have a significant influence on Sierra Leone, and for many years, I have actively promoted the country's culture. As a young lady born of African parents, I believe I have a distinct edge and can act as a link between the two cultures.

As a former active-duty member of the U.S Air Force who honorably served for 4 years, I am a strong advocate for women and girls in Sierra Leone. My passion for helping others and devotion to the service of humanity was crystalized after I made my first visit to Sierra Leone in 2003 and realized the tremendous need to help rebuild a fragile nation which still harbors the trappings of instability. Since then, I've worked tirelessly to raise the consciousness of Americans and the Global Community to the plight of women and girls in Sierra Leone. At the same time, I am working to sensitize, uplift, and reinforce women in Sierra Leone to role model as "actors of change," - a key ingredient that ensures social inclusion, gender equality and peace building. This framework emphasizes that engagement with Civil Society working on girls and women's rights should inform country level programs, regardless of the sector.

One of my greatest personal achievements is being a mother to two beautiful children, Jonathan, and Miriam. They are truly my pride and joy. I see myself in them both each day, physically and emotionally.

During both of my pregnancies, I experienced the worst nausea and was diagnosed with an ailment called *hyperemesis gravidarum* which caused me to vomit almost every single day for almost eight months. I feared that with all this extreme sickness, surely, I was bringing harm to my unborn children. But thankfully, both of my children were born healthy and strong. Thanks to Mother Nature's sense of humor, my children were born January 18th and January 20th, five years apart. Naturally, planning birthday parties have become an interesting ride as they get older. My focus is to plant the right seeds in my children so they can be an inspiration to the world. I try to always involve them in my service activities such as packing clothes to ship overseas or making encouragement cards. Unbeknown to them, my secret plan is to recruit them as Impact Sierra Leone interns someday soon. My proudest moment is when my son googled me and found many videos of me speaking at various events. He grabbed his sister and shouted, "Mom is a celebrity." I would have to say, I was a proud Mama Bear that day because I know my reputation made my children proud. I look forward to creating more memories with them as they are growing so fast. Motherhood has taught me and continues to teach me so much about myself and my character. Patience, Prayer, and planning are the keys to getting through motherhood and maintaining sanity. But it is a job I hold dearly and would not trade for the world. For in my children, I see two seeds that are growing each day but with lots of nourishment from their family circle.

    I am a mother to many, a philanthropist, a mentor, a health coach, a servant, and a motivational speaker. I am the Founder of Impact Sierra Leone, an organization founded to reduce socioeconomic challenges in Sierra Leone through empowerment, education, and building strong partnerships with the Diaspora community. I stand strong for the empowerment of Sierra Leoneans, African women, and children and for promoting the United Nations Sustainable Development Goals to rebuild our communities. I am a confident and charismatic woman who has won several awards and graced the cover of many empowerment magazines. It seems that the moment I truly fell in love with myself, flaws and all, that's when my true beauty was revealed and using my voice positively motivated me. I no longer accept the negative opinions of others.

How did I evolve from an insecure young lady into a confident, courageous, and unstoppable woman? Here are a few ways: Embrace self-love everyday- completely fall in love with yourself and who God created you to be in this world. I was careful to be kind to myself in my thoughts and actions. Use your social media platform to promote positive energy and share positive content that's inspiring. Take pride in your appearance and invest in it the best you can so you'll feel good about yourself. Develop healthy routines and habits like regular walking, eating more fruits and vegetables and loads of water. Remember: you are your own brand; market yourself each day through your speech, what you wear, what you post, and more. Determine your life goals and mission then connect your brand to this daily. Finally, find a cause to champion using your gifts, talents, and skills. By doing so, you will never have time to be insecure or focus on the wrong things.

There is so much power in our collective voices to break down barriers in leadership. But we must do a very important thing. We must raise this voice to see the change we want to see! I remember while in college, I took my first public speaking class while attending the Air Force Community College at Andrews Air Force Base. I tried my best to avoid this class, but it was a mandatory requirement for my two-year degree. I was then introduced to the world of social media in a great way. I learned from many mentors that there was power in using your voice and telling your story,

I realized that there are so many whose voices that can't be heard, not all by choice but most by just their circumstance. For this reason, I find joy in using my voice and platform to tell the stories, I have a responsibility to be their voice at every chance. By using our voices, we empower others to reach their highest potential and succeed on the stage, in the boardroom, in various industries, in our businesses, our organizations, and as entrepreneurs. I stand as a woman empowered with so many voices of other powerful men and women leaders. There is a voice that led them to be etched in history for their leadership, bravery, and courage.

- It is this voice that led **Harriet Tubman** *to the Underground Railroad.*

- It is this voice that inspired **Mother Teresa**, *a true humanitarian, to help so many people with such a selfless heart.*

- It is this voice that led **Fannie Lou Hamer** *to relentlessly fight for the rights of Mississippi voters.*

- It is this voice that made **Rosa Parks** *say enough is enough and ignited the Montgomery Bus Boycott.*

-It is this voice that inspired **Dr. Martin Luther King's** *I Have a Dream Speech.*

-It is this voice that inspired **Oumou Sangare**, *a native of Mali and a powerful singer who used her vocals to give voice to women in male-dominated communities.*

- It is this voice that inspired **Miriam Makeba** *to use her voice to address apartheid and unify the people of South Africa.*

-It is this voice that inspired **John F. Kennedy's** *inaugural address where he stated, "Ask not what your country can do for you, ask what you can do for your country!"*

--It is this voice that allowed **Kamala Harris** *to stand boldly and become the first female Vice President of the United States.*

--It is this voice that completely stopped the silence of one of the greatest poets in our history, a woman who at a young age was raped and went mute for years. None other than **Maya Angelou** *who without her gift, I could now declare that "Still I Rise".*

-It is the voice of my mother, **Harriett Memuna Sesay**, *who always reminded me that I was something special in the world and to always be a light in the world showing kindness and compassion.*

One thing several of the men and women I mentioned have in common is that they have used their voices to break down barriers! Sometimes it is your own voice that pushes you to your greatest potential. Finding my voice allowed me the courage to write this book with my heart, mind, and soul.

Conclusion

Someone once asked me what I would tell my younger self of 15-20 years ago. I would tell my younger youth to recognize her worth every single day. In doing so, my younger me would have made better life decisions and become an agent of change much sooner. When a woman knows her worth, recognizes her value, most insecurities are diminished and there is no fear of being yourself.

I would also seek a mentor earlier in life. Having solid mentors can encourage professional growth and lead you to your destiny. I would also tell my younger youth to find her voice which helped her discover her inner strength to overcome life's journey.

I have also been asked by several individuals to give advice on being a servant leader. I thought it would be great to share these life lessons for those wanting to live a life of service. The first piece of advice I offer is to search your heart for your true purpose. Discover what truly makes you happy. Search for a cause that does not seem like work but drives your passion daily. Serve without expectations. The reward is to see the needs of the people you are serving met. Build great friendships with those who serve with you because great relationships mean great service! Remember your 'WHY", the reason you are doing this work. No matter what, seize every opportunity to better yourself and to give back to your community. Don't live in regret but instead use your voice and your platform to impact lives because in doing so you are helping others win. Your voice is your victory, remember that! I recently came up with the following quote, "Give her wings to rise and she will soar above all defeats." Using my voice has given me wings to soar in an unstoppable way.

In life, it is very easy to be saturated in all the negative experiences that have happened in our lives, but we must not forget about positive experiences. To the young Africans in the U.S and Africa, I would encourage you to always remember there is power in the unity and voice of the youth. For first-generation born Africans, we must use our influence, our connections, our energies, and our skills to help our countries in any way. As African descendants, we have the honor of knowing our roots and making our ancestors proud by giving back. Our serving as a bridge between Africa and the Diaspora can bring much-needed resources and provide an opportunity for us to exchange cultural traditions and promote togetherness.

I went from voiceless Adama to victorious Adama, and I have not looked back. My failures and setbacks have become my greatest motivation to succeed. There are many

Conclusion

voices that have been silenced by death. It is up to us who are in the land of the living to embrace the gift of life and use our voices in a mighty way!

Bonus Recipes from Sierra Leone

Sierra Leonean culture is rich in cuisine. Throughout the years, I have enjoyed partaking in and cooking a variety of dishes. Preparing food for others is a labor of love. Because we are not in one another's presence, I wanted to share recipes for some of the most popular, delicious dishes from Sierra Leone with you. I hope that you and your loved ones will enjoy them together.

Krain Krain Soup

MAIN INGREDIENTS

Pepper

Meat or fish (of your choice)

Palm oil (3 cooking spoon or more)

Dried or smoked fish (of choice)

Crayfish (3 tablespoons)

Onion (1 chopped bulb)

Red or yellow flesh peppers

Stock cubes (to taste)

Salt (to taste)

Bitter leaf, pumpkin leaf, uziza leaf or utazi leaf

These are the ingredients used in the process of cooking the Krain Krain: pepper, onions, jumbo Maggie, season salt, all-purpose season, barracuda fish, chicken turkey, goat meat, palm oil, krain krain leaf, ogiri (sesame seed) and of course water. Prior to cooking, complete preparation such as picking, cleaning and cutting the krain krain, meat, pepper, onions, and the rest of the ingredients that you want.

Krain Krain can be cooked in different methods. Put water in the pot. Blend/grind/pound the pepper and onions together and pour it in the pot of water. Add palm oil and ogiri. Add your seasons and magie. Leave it to boil or cook for 20 to 30 minutes for taste and for the water to reduce a little in the pot because krain krain doesn't require a lot of water. After some time and you feel the water is less add the krain krain leaf in the pot and add slices of onions on top of the krain krain and cover the pot and reduce the fire. Allow it to steam for 5 to 10 minutes and mix in order to make sure it's not burning. Keep mixing with fire reduced, check for taste until you are able to achieve the end result. Serve with rice or fufu.

Sierra Leonean Cassava Leaves

MAIN INGREDIENTS
2 bundles of cassava leaves (or pounded frozen leaves)
1 lb meat
2 dried fish
1 cup cooked beans

½ pint palm oil/coconut or vegetable oil
½ cup peanut butter
1 large onion
2 red peppers
2 cups water

Cut up the meat and place in a saucepan with salt, ground pepper, onions and water. Cook for about 15 minutes. Wash leaves, beat in a mortar until finely ground. Defrost if you are using frozen pounded cassava leaves. Add the ground (or defrosted) leaves to the ingredients in the saucepan and simmer for about 10 minutes. Add palm oil and simmer again for about 10 minutes or until the meat is tender. Mix peanut butter with a little water and add to the sauce, stirring frequently to prevent burning. Flake fish and add together with cooked beans to the sauce. Season with salt, cover and simmer gently until most of the water has evaporated. Serve with rice.

Sierra Leonean Potato Leaves

MAIN INGREDIENTS
3 packs of already chopped sweet potato leaves
200ml of Palm oil
Pack of Ogiri

Tin of Butter beans

4 tablespoons Peanut butter (smooth)

Assorted meat of your choice

Smoked fish

Scotch bonnet pepper (to your taste)

2 medium sized Onions

Maggie seasoning (2 cubes)

Salt (to your taste)

Chop and wash potato leaves. Prepare a pot to boil meat with onion, pepper, and ogiri paste. Start with washing then bring your meat to boil until tender for approximately 30-40 minutes. Wash the chopped potato leaves and leave them in a colander to drain any excess water. Blend onions and scotch pepper with ogiri. This should look like a thick smooth paste. After the meat has boiled, add the above paste mixture and your meat in a medium sized cooking pot, add 2 pints of water and bring to a boil for about 20 minutes. While the pot boils, mix the peanut butter with 50ml of water so it is slightly watery. Add peanut butter mixture, palm oil, maggie seasoning, and salt after 20 minutes or until you have a thick soupy consistency. Then add the washed potato leaves with the smoked fish. Mix the pot and leave pot to boil for a further 15min in medium heat. Turn the heat low and let the sauce simmer for a further 5 min or until the palm oil is floating. Voila! Dish is done!

Okro or Okra Soup

(FRYING METHOD)

Okro soup is also known as draw soup, okra soup or lady's finger soup. Okro soup and ogbono soup are from the same family of draw soup. This delicious soup is made specifically for one to two days. Okro is a special vegetable that is enjoyed by all. This soup can go with any of the various types of vegetable leaves. Ogbono can be added to this okro soup to enhance its drawness. Okro is a versatile vegetable that goes with any protein. Okro soup is a versatile soup that goes with any swallow. Okro soup is the only soup that you can use meat and fresh iced fish together to cook the soup.

OKRO RECIPES

Okro as a vegetable, can be used to cook the following soup recipes: Okro soup, stew, Miyan kubewa. fisherman soup (to garnish)

MAIN INGREDIENTS

Okro (300g or 30 pieces)

Meat or fish (of your choice)
Palm oil (3 cooking spoon or more)
Dried or smoked fish (of choice)
Crayfish (3 tablespoons)
Onion (1 chopped bulb)
Red or yellow flesh peppers
Stock cubes (to taste)
Salt (To taste)
Bitter leaf, pumpkin leaf, uziza leaf or utazi leaf

OPTIONAL INGREDIENTS
Stockfish (1 big sized)
Prawns or shrimps (fresh or dry)
Cow skin (choice of amount)
Ogiri okpei (locust beans) 1 wrap
Fresh iced fish (any type)
Ogbono (100g ground)
Snails (8 big sized)
Periwinkles (removed or unremoved) 1 cup

ALTERNATIVE INGREDIENTS
Bitter leaf, pumpkin leaf, uziza leaf or utazi leaf
Dried or smoked fish
Meat or fresh fish (or both)
Prawns or shrimps (fresh or dry)

Red or yellow peppers

Dry or fresh peppers

Unremoved or Removed periwinkles (big size)

Frying method: This is the cooking method, whereby you start with the frying of the okro. This is the modern way of cooking okro soup and it is much sweeter than the traditional way of cooking this soup. With this method, the soup will not really draw.

Wash and chop/slice your okro with a knifeu or grater into big pieces. Note: The smaller its slices, the more it will draw. You can even pound the okro if you want it to draw very well. Pluck, wash, and shred your vegetable leaves of choice. Wash the removed/unremoved periwinkles, dried or smoked fish, stock fish and other ingredients and set them aside. Chop your onion and set it aside. Grind/blend your peppers and crayfish, separately and set them aside. Steam your meat/fish and other ingredients and set them aside. Roughly chop your tomatoes and set it aside.

Pour your palm oil into a dry empty cooking pot and once the oil is hot, add the chopped onion and fry on low heat for 3 minutes or until the onion becomes translucent. Add in your fresh ground/chopped pepper, chopped fresh tomatoes, ogiri and some ground crayfish and fry for like 3 minutes on low heat. (Only if you are using any of the ingredients.) Add the chopped/grated okro into the frying pot, fry on low heat and stir vigorously for about 2 to 4 minutes to start the drawing process. Then add in the meat/fish stock bit by bit and stir till it starts drawing. Note: If the meat/fish stock is exhausted and you feel that the soup is still thick, you can start by adding hot water, till you get the consistency of your choice. Add in the meat, and other ingredients you steamed with the meat, except the dried/smoked fish. You can now add the remaining ground crayfish into the cooking soup. If your choice of vegetable is bitter leaf, add and cover for 5 minutes without stirring it. Note: This step is only done if you are using bitter leaves. Add in your smoked fish or dried fish and removed/unremoved periwinkles. Taste for salt and other spices. You can now add water bit by bit to your own consistency of your choice and let it cook for 2 - 3 minutes. Note: This step is optional. If you are using pumpkin leaf, ugwu leaves, uziza leaves or utazi leaves, this is the right time; cover the pot and allow to simmer for 2 to 3 minutes. Note: Always make sure your pumpkin leaf is half done. Turn off the heat and your delicious okro soup is ready.

Jollof Rice

MAIN INGREDIENTS

Green peas

Green bean

Carrots

Cabbage (optional)

Bulb onions

Green pepper

Sweet corn

Fresh pepper

Curry and Thyme

Fried rice spice (you can also use turmeric)

Salt

Vegetable oil

Seasoning

Rice

Liver (optional)

Chicken

Dice all the vegetables (carrots, cabbage, green pepper, bulb onion and spring onion...) Par boil your chicken. Wash rice and parboil it. Cook the rice with the sauce from your parboiled chicken. Add your curry and thyme, salt, seasoning, fried rice spice and water (you can use turmeric also) to the rice. Stir altogether and cook over low heat. Steam the vegetables, pepper, etc. in a small pan or pot (you can add a pinch of salt and seasoning). When the rice is ready, pour the steamed veggies, pepper, etc. into the pot containing your rice and stir or you can mix them beat by beat.

Your fried rice is ready.

Fufu

I must say, making fufu at home yourself from scratch is not for the faint-hearted. It requires some arm work, but it is totally worth it especially if you live in the diaspora. It is not what I will make every week because of the huge amount of energy expended while making it.

Cassava FuFu

Add the cassava dough/pulp into a heavy bottom pot, break the pulp into smaller pieces with your hands. Add water and mix to combine with your hand until lump free and a smooth paste is achieved. The consistency would be like that of thick double cream. Turn on the heat to medium-low heat and start stirring vigorously, the fufu will start changing color from white to off white. You will have to keep stirring to combine. The fufu will become hard to stir and feel stretchy at some point, you will need to add warm water to the mix as needed. Cover the pan pot with its lid and leave to cook for about 5 to 10 minutes so that the steam can cook the fufu thoroughly and desired softness is achieved. You will know the fufu is cooked through when it is no longer white; the final result will be an off-white in color. Portion the cooked fufu into bowls or in cling film until you are ready to use. Serve with any soup of choice.

Pepper Chicken

For marination:
1 kg chicken
1 tbsp pepper powder
2 tbsp Lemon Juice ½ tsp salt

MAIN INGREDIENTS
2 medium yellow onions (about 12 ounces; 340g), halved and ends trimmed, divided
2 cups (480ml) homemade or store-bought low-sodium chicken broth, plus more as needed, divided
5 medium cloves garlic, divided
1 ounce (28g) fresh ginger (about a 1-inch knob), divided
2 teaspoons tomato paste

4 bone-in, skin-on chicken legs (about 2 pounds; 900g)

1 hot chili pepper, such as bird's eye, habanero, or Scotch bonnet (see note)

2 bay leaves

1 cup creamy peanut butter (9 ounces; 255g)

1 (28-ounce; 794g) can plum tomatoes

1 whole smoke-dried fish, such as tilapia or snapper (see note)

Kosher salt and freshly ground black pepper

Pair with white rice or fufu

      In a blender, purée 2 onion halves, 1/2 cup (120ml) chicken stock, 3 garlic cloves, 1/2 ounce ginger, and tomato paste. In a Dutch oven, combine chicken legs with purée, remaining onion halves, remaining 1/2 ounce ginger, and remaining 2 cloves garlic, along with hot pepper and bay leaves. Toss to coat. Set Dutch oven over medium heat and bring to a simmer, then cover, reduce heat to low, and cook until halved onion is soft and translucent, about 20 minutes. Add an extra 1/2 cup (120ml) chicken stock if mixture begins to stick to the bottom of the pot. Transfer chunks of onion, ginger, garlic cloves, and hot pepper to blender. Add peanut butter, canned tomatoes and their juices, and remaining 1 1/2 cups (360ml) chicken stock and purée until smooth. Pass blended mix through a fine-mesh strainer into the Dutch oven, stirring to incorporate. Increase heat to medium and bring to a simmer, then lower heat to medium-low and cook, stirring occasionally, until chicken is tender, oils have surfaced, and mixture has thickened and reduced by about one-third, about 40 minutes. Add smoked fish, reduce heat to low, cover pot, and cook an additional 5 minutes. (If omitting the smoked fish, you can skip this 5-minute covered-cooking step.) Remove and discard smoked fish and bay leaves, season with salt and pepper to taste, and serve hot over white rice or fufu.

About the Author

Motivational speaker, author, women's empowerment leader, and global humanitarian, Dr Adama Kalokoh, is an African woman and changemaker excelling in a multitude of fields and industries. She is a Chairperson of the Global Goodwill Ambassadors Foundation (GGAF), a Sustainable Development Goals (SDG) advocate, and the Founder of Impact Sierra Leone, which she started in 2019 to reduce socioeconomic challenges in Sierra Leone through empowerment, education, and building strong partnerships within the diaspora community.

Dr. Kalokoh, a proud descendant of Sierra Leone,

has always had a passion for helping others and international development. Her parents instilled in her a deep sense of pride and appreciation for their Sierra Leonean heritage. As a former active-duty member of the U.S Air Force who honorably served for 4 years, Dr. Kalokoh is a strong advocate for women and girls in Sierra Leone. She received an honorary Doctor of Philosophy degree from Oved Dei Seminary Institute for her global missionary work. She hopes that her mission will inspire other descendants of Africa to embrace their culture and positively impact their home country.

Dr. Kalokoh completed her undergraduate studies at the University of the District of Columbia majoring in public health and holds a Bachelor of Science in health education. Her leadership development began as a recipient of the Thurgood Marshall Scholarship while at the university.

Upon the conclusion of her education, Dr. Kalokoh was inducted into the AmeriCorps Promise Fellowship (2001-2003) and served as a Volunteer Director. Her leadership led her to reach thousands of marginalized people at soup kitchens, shelters, and schools in the DC area. But her passion for Sierra Leone became a driving force.

About the Author

Her current efforts include directly supporting a rural community in Sierra Leone with educational tools, clothes donations, and support for farming activities. Using her passion for public health, she launched Impact Sierre Leone's anchor program, the Seeds of Life, in March 2021 to combat hunger amongst primary school children in the village and it has now expanded to six projects. She hopes to continue serving humanity through her missionary works and launch several other projects that promote literacy, public health, enhanced education, empowerment, mentorship and more that will bring lasting solutions to poverty issues. She hopes to grow Impact Sierra Leone into a Global brand that will transform the lives of many.

Honors

Here are some of my professional accomplishments that I am most grateful and honored to receive but more importantly, they came to fruition after I opened my voice and used it to change lives:

- Recipient of The White House Presidential Lifetime Achievement Medal for her humanitarian service in 2023, nominated by the Jacobs Abbey Global Institute for Leadership Institute (JAGILS).

- Received a 2023 African Community Service Award (ACSA) for my commitment to improving the lives of underserved communities.
- Honored and received recognition in Sierra Leone and the U.S as the Yonibana Brand Ambassador, Female Empowerment Entrepreneur, 2019 Yoni Excellence Diasporan of the Year, 2019 DDEA Humanitarian Recipient, chosen as a 2019 Global Goodwill Ambassador, was among the Top 100 Recognized Human Rights Defenders in the United Nations 2019 Almanac
- Received the 2021 Nina L. Meyerhof Leadership Award for humanitarian service. This award recognizes outstanding individuals who dedicate their lives to bring positive social change and devote their time to fighting poverty, injustice and whose accomplishments are consistent with Jacobs-Abbey Global Institute for Leadership Studies goals. In addition, her commanding personality has made her a natural for hosting a series of successful fundraising events through collaboration with the community association and church organizations in the DC area between 2004 and 2020.
- Received Special Recognition Award from The City Scope Africa (CSA) organization at the 2022 African

About the Author

Business Professions and Entrepreneurs Conference (October 2022)

- Women's Empowerment award- Recognized by the Center for Truth and Healing for my efforts to empower women in Sierra Leone, West Africa (March 2022)
- Recognized by Business Africa Online (BAO) as one of 30 Inspiring Women who are #BreakingThe Bias (March 2022)
- Received the Prize of Peace Award for The Children's Aid and Help by the Federation of International Gender and Human Rights (December 2020)
- Recognized by Humanitarian Awards Global (HAG) as one of the Most Distinguished Change Makers: Women In Africa 2020-2021
- Received a SHE Impacts Award by Talk Love Foundation for my social development and humanitarian work (March 2022)
- Received official Chaplain's license from the Global Oved Dei Seminary & University (August 2020)
- Received certification as a My Body Is My Body (MBIMB) ambassador from the Global Goodwill

Ambassadors Foundation to promote child safety (February 2021)
- Featured in a special edition of the Global Goodwill Ambassador Magazine: for International Women's Day (March 2022)
- Featured in the Formidable Woman Magazine by Celebrity Writer in 2019 n for my work with women/girl's empowerment
- Featured in the African Eye Report in 2021 with a featured article: Empowering the Next Generation of Sierra Leoneans (Masahudu Ankiilu Kunateh)
- Recognized by City Scope on Women's Crush Wednesday for my work in Women/Girls Empowerment
- Served as judge for the Hult Prize ILEAD (Institute of Leadership, Entrepreneurship and Development) On Campus Competition
- Contributing author to the Credentials of Entrepreneur Book (28 COE) May 2021)
- Received a humanitarian leadership award from the DDEA organization (September 2019)
- Received recognition from the Cuento Conmigo as an Ambassador for solidarity and sustainability for promoting the SDGs (March 2020)

About the Author

- Contributing author in the Amazon Bestseller Book: "A Woman's Guide to Business Domination with Annie Gibbons (September 2022) with my featured Chapter: "Creating Your Unique Value Proposition"
- Campaign Manager for Sia Finoh- 2022 Candidate for Prince Georges County Council District 3
- Mother to two beautiful children, Jonathan (16 years) and Miriam (11 years)
- Veteran of the United States Air Force, Honorable Discharge

Motivational Speaking Engagements

- Speaker and Presenter at the City Scope Africa (CSA) organization at the 2022 African Business Professions and Entrepreneurs Conference (October 2022) with the theme: Expanding Business Horizons: Capacity Building and Reliability in the Human Capitol
- Speaker and Presenter at the August 2022 Career Employability and Enterprise Leadership (CEEL) Well Global Summer Series Conference with a feature presentation entitled: Pattern of Success- Building Global Woman Leadership

- Featured guest speaker at the Rotaract Mount Aureole Weekly Series with the theme: Empowered to Lead: There is a Leader in all of us
- Featured guest speaker on the Scholars for Change Series (SAEL) Change Makers Forum (April 2021)
- Featured guest speaker on the African Seasoned Speakers Network with the theme: The Power of Impact and topic- Being a Game Change (September 2022)
- Featured speaker at the Women's Biz Tribe Success Summit speaking on the topic: The Power of My Voice (September 2022)
- Featured guest speaker at the See America in Color: Friday Night Flights Series with the theme: Make Civics Count (April 2021)
- Featured speaker at the International Women's Day 2021 event led by the Jacobs Abbey Global Institute for Leadership Studies with the theme topic: Challenge the Status Quo; Breaking the Glass Ceiling
- Featured guest speaker on the "Real Talk Real Solutions Show with Dr. Anana- Women and Youth Civility Practitioner
- Speaker and Presenter at the Lady Politico Power Global Leadership Conference with theme: Women

About the Author

in Politics-The Barriers in Participation and Leadership (March 8-9th, 2022) My featured topic presented was The Power of Finding Your Voice as a Global Woman Leader

- Speaker and Presenter at the 2022 Rise of Africa Virtual Conference with Clarence Cole and Honorable Clyde Rivers (August 20th)
- Featured Speaker as a Women in Leadership by DP Global Ministries (April 2021)-The Leadership Conversation
- Featured Speaker and Presenter at Speak Life 2 The Nations (July 2020)
- Featured Speaker and presenter at the Nkabom Journey for Peace and Development Event (March 2021) with the theme: The impact of politically induced conflicts and wars on the lives of women and children.
- Speaker and presenter at the Globa Goodwill Ambassador (GGA) Youth Global Change Cohort (August 2020)
- Speaker at the Sierra Leone Model African Union National Launching Ceremony (June 2021)

- Speaker and Presenter at the International Civility for the Girl Child Day: My Voice, Our Future (October 2020)
- Speaker and Presenter at the International Civility of the Girl Child Day with the Theme- It's Now O'clock (October 2022)
- Featured Speaker/Panelist on Dr. Ruby's Talk Show: "Empower with Your Story Series" (August 2022)
- Featured Speaker at the People of Impact Discussion on Imagination in Empowering Children (September 2022)
- Featured Speaker at the Kuntrol Global Conference for the "Voice Against Racism and Rape" (June 2020)
- Received Honorary Doctor of Philosophy from the Global Oved dei Seminary University for my missionary and humanitarian service (August 2020)

Favorite Affirmations

I am inspired to inspire has always been my favorite affirmation. It simply means that I feel deeply we were all created to be an inspiration to others. I try my best to exude inspiration in every way by using my voice, especially in my

About the Author

leadership roles. Being an inspiration reminds me of the brightest sun shining for the whole world to feel the warmth. Here are some of my personalized quotes that I hope leave you inspired:

Use your gifts and talents to inspire the world.
Creativity is the best way to stay motivated.
An attitude of gratitude increases your latitude in life.
Make your yesterday better than your today.
A great attitude is your best wardrobe.
No matter the challenges, take time to breathe.
Pull Out the I will in your Life daily.
Live out each day with passion and purpose.
Be kind to yourself mentally and physically.
Be someone else's sunshine.
You don't need a degree to be a mentor.
Greatness lives inside of you.
Remember who you are and embrace your roots.
Humanity and compassion always win.
Be determined to be your best every day.
Never stop learning and growing.
Your life is like an open book. Be sure each chapter is unforgettable!
Positive thinking will lead you to your greatest potential.

Create a legacy that will impact the future generation.

Turn your problems into your power!

Let Kindness be your superpower.

A true leader always serves others.

An empowered girl can change her community & the whole world.

Be empowered to inspire the world!

You were created to do great things so make it happen.

Love yourself deeply so that you can love others from the heart.

Be a butterfly with wings always ready to rise above the winds of life.

Acknowledgements

I believe in the value of great relationships. Networking with the right people and developing great mentorship relationships has been a major key to my journey to success. I've been fortunate to come across many great individuals who recognized my passion for humanity and community service and have become supporters, donors, and mentors.

To name a few, Mrs. Pamela Luckett, Executive Director for Hope Worldwide Mid-Atlantic influenced me greatly when I was an AmeriCorps Fellow. She was technically my first boss but taught me so much about working with people and being excellent in my service; the late Mrs. Bernadette Kamara, Executive Director for Sierra Leone Relief and Development Outreach, who influenced me in changing lives in Sierra Leone and taught me how to be compassionate; Mr. David W. Anderson who played a major role in my professional development and taught me the value of good networking and nurturing my skills; the late Ambassador Foday Mansaray influenced me in achieving Sustainable Development Goals (SDG) as I defend the rights of the girl child; I learned the core values of leadership and service during my years in the U.S Air Force; and my parents without whom I would not exist in the world.

www.ingramcontent.com/pod-product-compliance
Lightning Source LLC
Chambersburg PA
CBHW072140160426
43197CB00012B/2186